LEE-ENFIELD RIFLE

Exploded Drawings and Parts List

Rifle No. 1 MARK II & Mark III (SMLE)
Rifle No. 3 (Pattern 14)
Rifle No. 4 Mark I and Mark I*

Frederic Faust

LEE- ENFIELD RIFLE
Exploded Drawings and Parts Listings
Rifle No. 1 MARK II & Mark III (SMLE)
Rifle No. 3 (Pattern 14)
Rifle No. 4 Mark I and Mark I*

Copyright © 2018 Frederic Faust - All rights reserved.

ISBN: 978-0934523-6-39

Editor@Middle-Coast-Publishing.com

"Good Books Are Where We Find Our Dreams" SM

Dedication

This book is dedicated to the heroic soldiers of the King and Queen, the Tommies who defended the British Empire while carrying Lee-Enfield rifles.

CONTENTS

Abbreviations

STANDARD ABBREVIATIONS FOR USE IN IDENTIFICATION LISTS

A.	Assembly
A.A.	Anti-Aircraft
Al.	Aluminium
A.P.	Armour Piercing
Asb.	Asbestos
Aust.	Australian Pattern
B.	Bronze
B.A.	British Association
Bel.	Bellite
Ber.	Beryllium
B.P.St.	Bullet Proof Steel
Br.	Brass
Brol.	Brolium
B.S.F.	British Standard Fine
B.S.W.	British Standard Whitworth
C.	Copper
Carb.	Carbon
C.F.P.	Cotton Filled Plastic
Ch.	Chrome
Ch.St.	Chrome Steel
Ch.hd.	Cheese Head
C.I.	Cast Iron
Ck.	Cork
Contd.	Continued
C.St.	Cast Steel
Csk.	Countersunk
Cvs.	Canvas
D.C.	Die Cast
Dfx.	Duraflex
Dia. or d.	Diameter
Dur.	Duralium
F.	Felt
Fi.	Fibre
Fil.Hd.	Fillet Head
Ft.	Foot or Feet
G.A.	General Arrangement
Galv.	Galvanised
Gl.	Glass
G.M.	Gun Metal
Hd.	Head
Hex.	Hexagonal
Hidu.	Hiduminium
H.Pd.	Hot Pressed
H.R.	Hard Rolled
H.T.S.	Heat Treated Steel
I.Hd.	Instrument Head
In. or "	Inches
Inst.	Instrument
L.	Leather
L.H.	Left Hand
M.A.	Main Assembly
M.B.	Manganese Bronze
M.C.I.	Malleable Cast Iron
Mk.	Mark
mm.	Millimetre
M.S.	Mild Steel
N.	Nickel
No.	Number
N.Sil.	Nickel Silver
Ny.	Nycase
Pa.	Paper
Ph.B.	Phosphor Bronze
Pl.	Plate
P.M.	Plastic Moulding
Porc.	Porcelain
Pr.	Pounder
Q.F.	Quick Firing
R.	Rubber
R.B.	Rolled Bronze
Rd.	Round
S.A.	Sub. Assembly
Sq.	Square
Sh.	Sheet
Si.	Silicon
Sil.	Silver
Slch.	Silichrome
S.M.G.	Sub. Machine Gun
S.S.	Spring Steel
Sta.St.	Stainless Steel
S.T.	Single Turn
St.	Steel
S.W.G.	Standard Wire Gauge
Vdum.	Vanadium
W.M.	White Metal

Key Plate
RIFLE No1 S.M.L.E. ·303 MK.III
(With Cut-Off)
A
B
C
RIFLE No1, S.M.L.E., ·303 MK.III*
RIFLE No1, S.M.L.E., ·303 EMERGENCY

Plate A

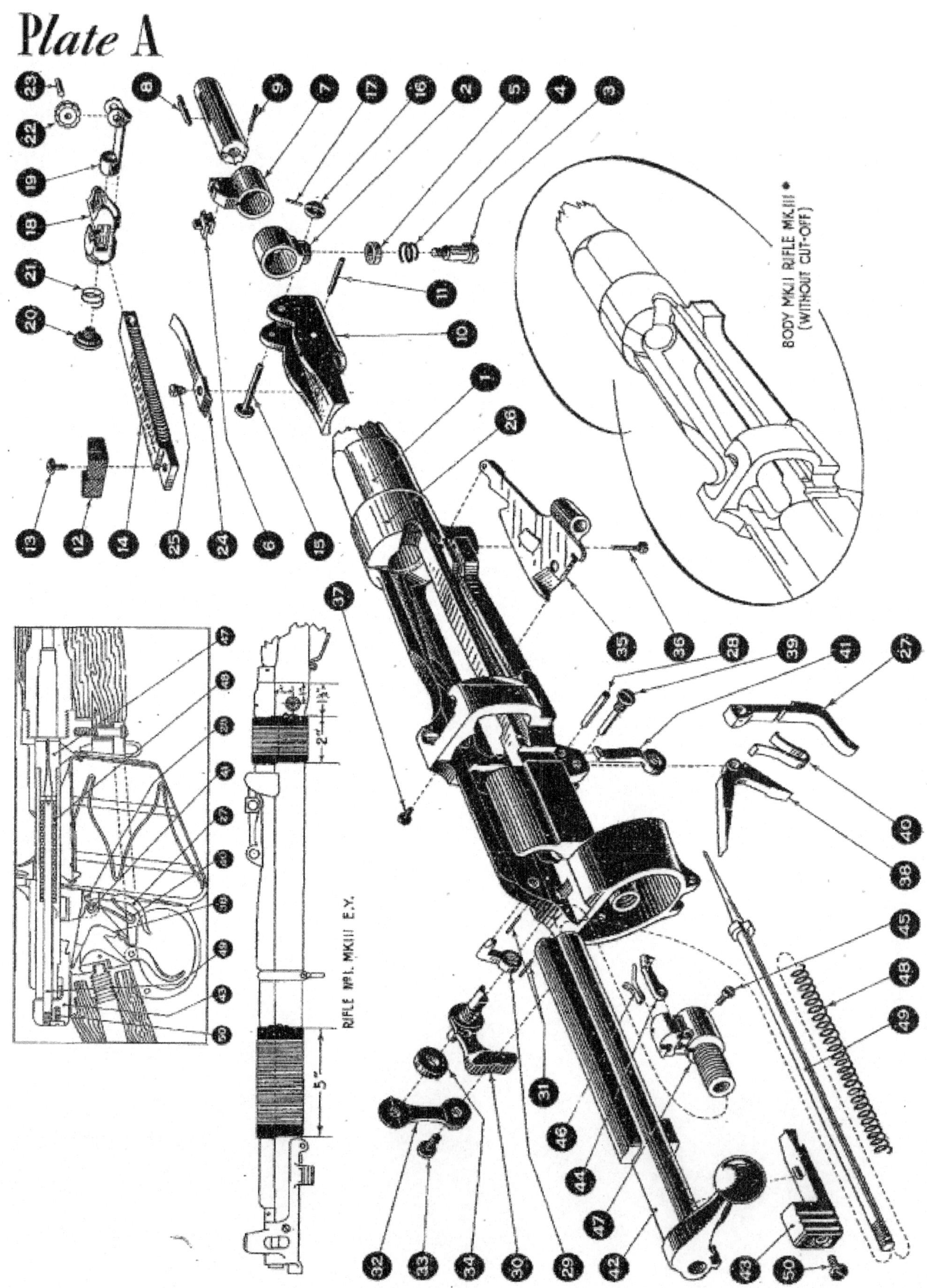

Rifle No. 1 Mark III and Mark III*

REF. NO.	DESIGNATION		VOCAB. NUMBER	MAT.	NO. OFF	DRAWING NUMBER
. . .	RIFLE, NO.1, MK.III., .303-in.		GA			SAID 1317
. . .	BARREL ASSEMBLY		A			" 1318
A 1	BARREL (a)			St.	1	" "
2	BAND, inner			St.	1	" "
3	SCREW	*	BB 0724	St.	1	" 1320
4	SPRING	*	" 0757	S.S.	1	" 1319
5	WASHER	*	" 0783	St.	1	" 1320
. . .	FORESIGHT		SA			" 1318
6	BLADE			St.	1	" "
	Sizes :- - .06"	*	BB 0654			" "
	- .045"	*	" 0655			" "
	- .03"	*	" 0656			" "
	- .015"	*	" 0657			" "
	"0"	*	" 0658			" "
	+ .015"	*	" 0659			" "
	+ .03"	*	" 0660			" "
	+ .045"	*	" 6145			" "
7	BLOCK, band	*	BAA 3403	St.	1	" "
8	KEY	*	" 3405	St.	1	" "
9	PIN, fixing	*	" 3406	St.	1	" 1320
. . .	BODY ASSEMBLY		A			
. . .	BACKSIGHT		SA			" 1318
10	BED	*	" 3401	St.	1	" "
11	PIN, fixing	*	" 3407	St.	1	" 1320
12	CAP (b)	*	BB 0665	St.	1	" 1318
13	SCREW (c)	*	" 0726	St.	1	" 1320
14	LEAF, "B" (d)	*	" 0696	St.	1	" 1318
15	PIN, axis	*	" 0706	St.	1	" 1320
16	WASHER	*	" 0781	St.	1	" "
17	PIN	*	" 0716	St.	1	" "
18	SLIDE	*	" 0747	St.	1	" 1318
19	CATCH	*	" 0672	St.	1	" "
20	SCREW	*	" 0730	St.	1	" 1320
21	SPRING	*	" 0751	S.S.	1	" 1319
22	WORM	*	" 0786	St.	1	" 1318
23	PIN	*	" 0717	St.	1	" 1320
24	SPRING, sight back	*	" 0760	S.S.	1	" 1319
25	SCREW	*	" 0741	St.	1	" 1320
	(a) Barrel, without body, with sights	*	BAA 3400			
	(b) Cap, backsight, (Aust)	*	" 3404			
	(c) Screw, cap, backsight, (Aust)	*	" 3113			
	(d) Leaf, backsight, (Aust)	*	" 3406			
	Notes (b), (c) and (d) are used on Rifles manufactured since 1943.					

Plate A

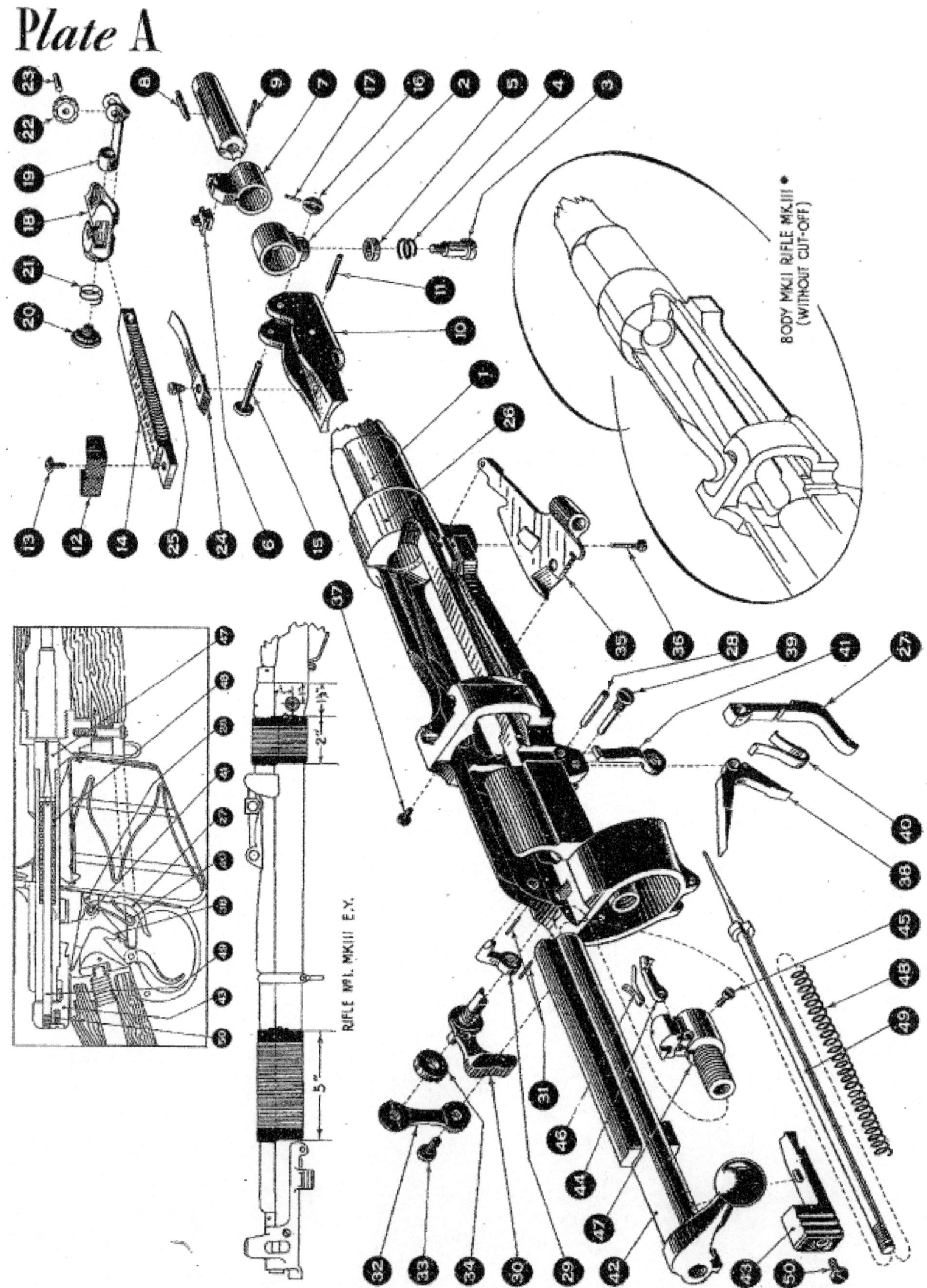

REF. NO.	DESIGNATION			VOCAB. NUMBER	MAT	NO. OFF	DRAWING NUMBER
. . .	RIFLE, NO.1, MK.III.,.303-in. (continued)						
. . .	BODY ASSEMBLY (continued)						
A 26	BODY			BB 0595	St.	1	SAID 1318
27	CATCH, magazine		*	BB 0670	St.	1	" "
28	PIN		*	" 0707	St.	1	" 1320
29	CATCH, safety		*	" 0671	St.	1	" 1318
30	BOLT, locking		*	" 0662	St.	1	" "
31	PIN, stop		*	" 0713	St.	2	" 1320
32	SPRING, Mk.I.	(a)	*	" 0750	St.	1	" 1319
33	SCREW, Mk.I.	(b)	*	" 0740	St.	1	" 1320
34	WASHER, Mk.I.	(c)	*	" 0784	St.	1	" "
35	CUT-OFF				St.	1	
36	SCREW				St.	1	
37	SCREW, ejector, "B"		*	" 0733	St.	1	" "
38	SEAR		*	" 0746	St.	1	" 1318
39	SCREW		*	" 0739	St.	1	" 1320
40	SPRING		*	" 0759	S.S.	1	" 1319
41	SPRING, retaining		*	" 0756	S.S.	1	" 1319
. . .	BOLT, BREECH, ASSEMBLY			SA			" 1318
42	BOLT		*	" 0661	St.	1	" "
43	COCKING-PIECE, "B"		*	" 0675	St.	1	" "
44	EXTRACTOR		*	" 0680	St.	1	" "
45	SCREW		*	" 0734	St.	1	" 1320
46	SPRING		*	" 0732	S.S.	1	" 1319
47	HEAD		*	" 0690	St.	1	" 1318
48	SPRING, main		*	" 0754	S.S.	1	" 1319
49	STRIKER, "B"		*	" 0769	St.	1	" 1318
50	SCREW		*	" 0743	St.	1	" 1320
	(a) Also Spring, Mk.II.		*	BB 7951			
	(b) Also Screw, Mk.II. To be demanded as Screw, cap, backsight (Cat.No. BB 0726)		*				
	(c) Also Washer, Mk.II.		*	BAA 7931			
	Notes (a), (b) and (c) are used on Rifles manufactured since 1943.						

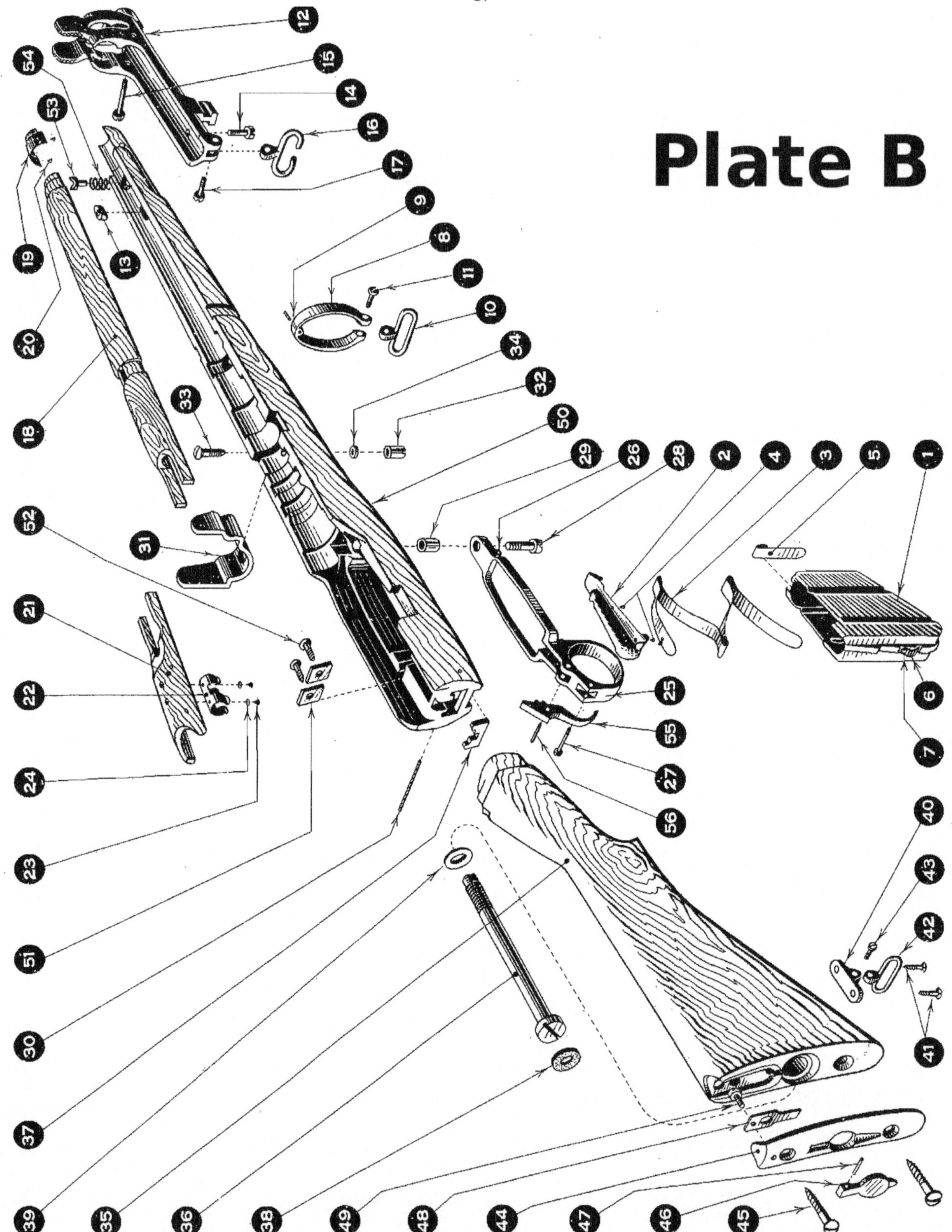
12
15
14
16
17
9
8
11
10
34
32
50
29
26
28
2
4
3
5
1
54
53
19
13
20
18
33
52
31
21
22
24
23
51
30
37
39
35
36
38
49
48
44
47
46
45
6
7
25
55
27
56
40
43
42
41

Plate B

RIFLE No. 1, Mk.III and Mk.III*

REF. NO.	DESIGNATION		VOCAB. NUMBER	MAT.	NO. OFF	DRAWING NUMBER	
. . .	RIFLE, NO.1, MK.III., .303-in., (continued)-						
. . .	MAGAZINE "B"	*	BB 0698 SA			SAID 1317	
B 1	CASE, "B"	*	" 0669	St.	1	" "	
2	PLATFORM, "B"	*	" 0721	St.	1	" "	
3	SPRING			S.S.	1	" 1319	
4	RIVET	*	BAA 3411	M.S.	2	" 1320	
5	SPRING, auxiliary, "B"	*	BB 0749	S.S.	1	" 1319	
6	SPRING, rib	*	BAA 3414	S.S.	1	" "	
7	RIVET	*	" 3412	M.S.	1	" 1320	
. . .	STOCK ASSEMBLY					" 1317	
8	BAND, outer	*	BB 0652	St.	1	" 1318	
9	PIN, joint	*	BAA 3409	St.	1	" 1320	
10	SWIVEL, sling	*	BP 0774	St.	(i) 1	" 1319	
11	SCREW	*	" 0744	St.	(i) 1	" 1320	
12	CAP, nose	*	" 0667	St.	1	" 1318	
13	NUT	*	" 0700	St.	1	" 1320	
14	SCREW, back	*	" 0728	St.	1	" "	
15	SCREW, front	*	" 0729	St.	1	" "	
16	SWIVEL, piling, "B"		" 0773	St.	1	" 1319	
17	SCREW		" 0744	St.	(i) 1	" 1320	
18	GUARD, hand, front	*	" 0685	Wood	1	" 1317	
19	CAP	*	" 0666	St.	1	" "	
20	SCREW	*	" 0727	St.	2	" 1320	
21	GUARD, hand, rear	*	" 0686	Wood	1	" 1317	
22	SPRING	*	" 0753	S.S.	1	" 1319	
23	RIVET	*	" 0723	C.	2	" 1320	
24	WASHER	*	" 0779	C.	2	" "	
25	GUARD, trigger	*	" 0687	St.	1	" 1318	
26	LOOP, cover, breech			St.	1	" "	
27	SCREW, back	*	" 0735	St.	1	" 1320	
28	SCREW, front	*	" 0736	St.	1	" "	
29	COLLAR	*	" 0676	St.	1	" 1319	

Plate B

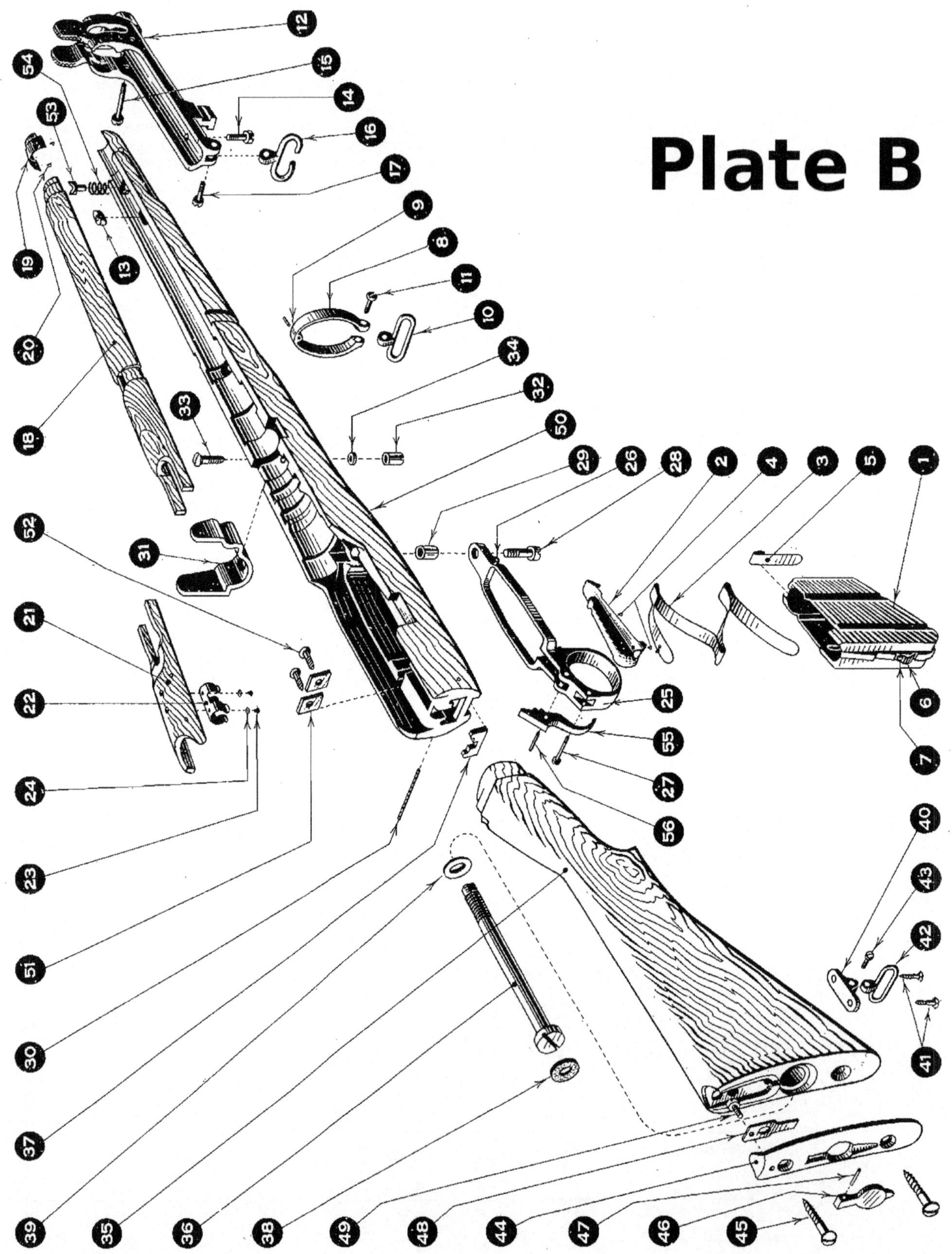

REF. NO.	DESIGNATION		VOCAB. NUMBER	MAT.	NO. OFF.	DRAWING NUMBER	
. . .	RIFLE, NO.1, MK.III., .303-in. (continued)						
. . .	STOCK ASSEMBLY (continued)						
B 30	PIN, screwed, fore-end			Br.	1	SAID 1320	
31	PROTECTOR	*	BB 0722	St.	1	" 1317	
32	NUT	*	" 0701	St.	1	" 1320	Ø STOCK, butt.
33	SCREW	*	" 0738	St.	1	" "	Sizes :-
34	WASHER, nut, screw	*	" 0780	St.	1	" "	Bantam BB 9764
35	STOCK, butt, Mk.I. Ø			Wood		" 1317	* * Long BB 0765
36	BOLT, "A"	*	" 0663	St.	1	" 1319	* Normal BB 0766
37	PLATE	*	" 0719	St.	1	" "	* Short BB 0767
38	WAD	*	" 0777	L.	1	" 1320	
39	WASHER	*	" 0778	St.	1	" "	
40	BRACKET	*	" 0664	St.	1	" 1318	
41	SCREW	*	" 0725	St.	2	" 1320	
42	SWIVEL, sling	*	" 0774	St.	(1) 1	" 1319	
43	SCREW	*	" 0744	St.	(1) 1	" 1320	
44	PLATE, butt (a)	*		Br.	1	" 1319	
45	SCREW	*	" 0737	St.	2	" 1320	
46	TRAP	*	" 0775	Br.	1	" 1318	
47	PIN	*	" 0714	St.	1	" 1320	
48	SPRING	*	" 0762	S.S.	1	" 1319	
49	SCREW	*	" 0742	St.	1	" 1320	
50	STOCK, fore-end "B"	*	" 0768	Wood	1	" 1317	
51	PLATE, copper (b)	*	BAA 3410	C.	2		
52	SCREW			Br.	2		
53	STUD	*	BB 0771	St.	1	" "	
54	SPRING	*	" 0761	S.S.	1	" 1319	
55	TRIGGER	*	" 0776	St.	1	" 1318	
56	PIN	*	" 0715	St.	(1) 1	" 1320	
	(a) Plate, butt, Assd.	*	BB 0718				
	(b) Includes screws						

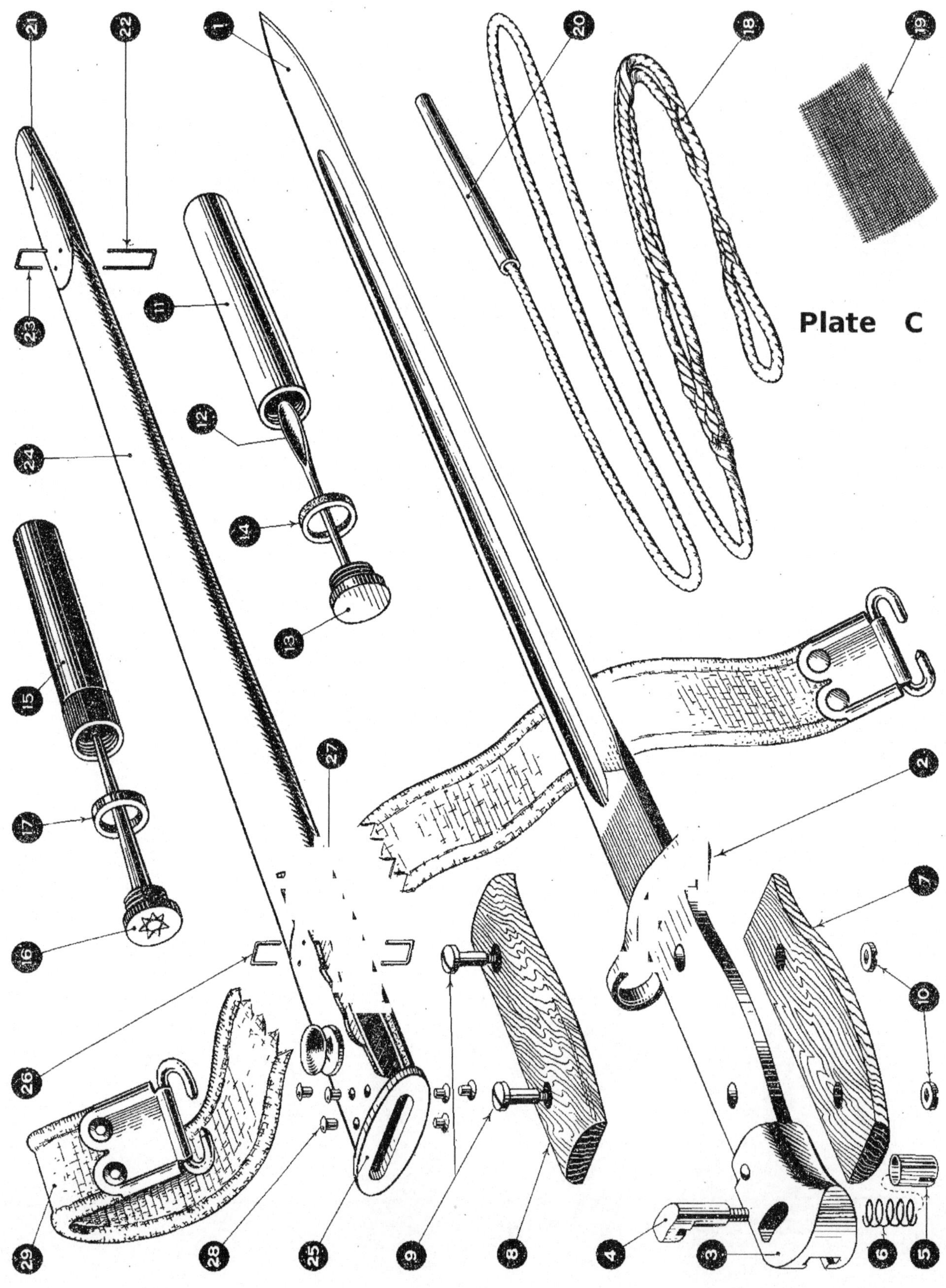

Plate C

REF. NO.	DESIGNATION		VOCAB. NUMBER	MAT.	NO. OFF	DRAWING NUMBER	
. . .	RIFLE, NO.1, MK.III., ACCESSORIES						
. . .	BAYONET, NO.1, MK.1.	*	BA 0022 A			SAID 2474	
C 1	BLADE			St.	1	" "	
2	CROSS-PIECE — Brazed to blade			St.	1	" "	
3	POMMEL — Brazed to blade			St.	1	" "	Ø Pull-through, single, Mk.IV, "A" BA 0517.
4	BOLT	*	BB 0024	St.	1	" "	
5	NUT	*	" 0033	St.	1	" "	
6	SPRING	*	" 0036	St.	1	" "	* Pull-through, single, Mk.IV, "B" BA 0518.
7	GRIP, left — pair	*	" 0025	Wood	1	" "	
8	GRIP, right — pair			Wood	1	" "	
9	SCREW, securing grip	*	" 0035	St.	2	" "	
10	NUT	*	" 0034	St.	2	" "	
. . .	BOTTLE, OIL, MK.IV.	*	BA 0053 A			ADD(S)360	
11	BODY			Br.	1	" "	
12	SPOON	*	BB 0054	St.	1	" 357	
13	STOPPER	*	" 0055	Br.	1	" 358	
14	WASHER	*	" 0056	L.	1	" 359	
. . .	or BOTTLE, OIL, MK.V.,	*	BA 6320 A			DD(E)2562	
15	BODY			P.M.	1	" " -1	
16	STOPPER, with rod	*	BB 6321	P.M.	1	" " -4	
17	WASHER	*	" 6326	L.	1	" " -3	
. . .	PULL-THROUGH, SINGLE, MK.IV., "A" or "B" Ø					SAID 2578	
18	CORD, single	*	" 0520	Cord	1	" "	
19	GAUZE (not provided with "B" pull-through)	*	" 0521	St.	1	" "	
20	WEIGHT	*	" 0522	Br.	1	" "	
. . .	SCABBARD, BAYONET, NO.1, MK.II.	*	BA 1211 A			" 2474	
21	CHAPE	*	BB 1212	St.		" "	
22	LACE, long, .056"dia.x 1.35"M.S. wire	*	" 1213	M.S.	1	" "	
23	LACE, short, .056"dia.x 1.05" M.S. wire	*	" 1214	M.S.	(i) 1	" "	
24	LEATHER	*	" 8353	L.		" "	
25	LOCKET	*	" 1216	St.	1	" "	
26	LACE, short, .056"dia.x 1.05" M.S. wire		" 1214	M.S.	(i) 2	" "	
27	SPRING			St.	2	" "	
28	RIVET			M.S.	6	" "	
29	SLING, rifle, web, (complete)		AA 1657	Web	1	" "	

RIFLE No. 3 MK.1* (T), ·303 IN. PATTERN 1914

complete with

SIGHT TELESCOPIC (AUST.) PATTERN 1918

and

BAYONET No.3 MK.1

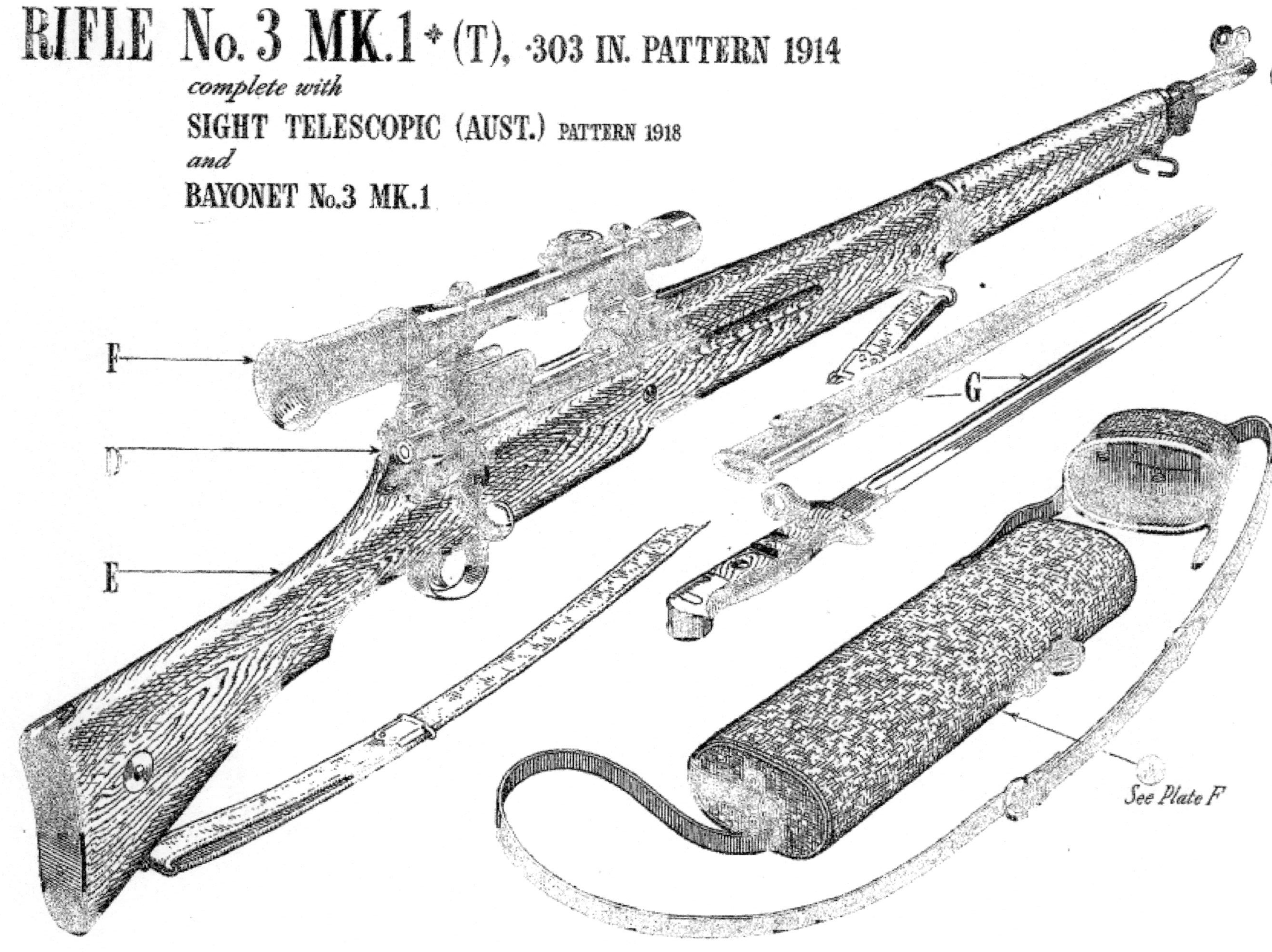

Plate D

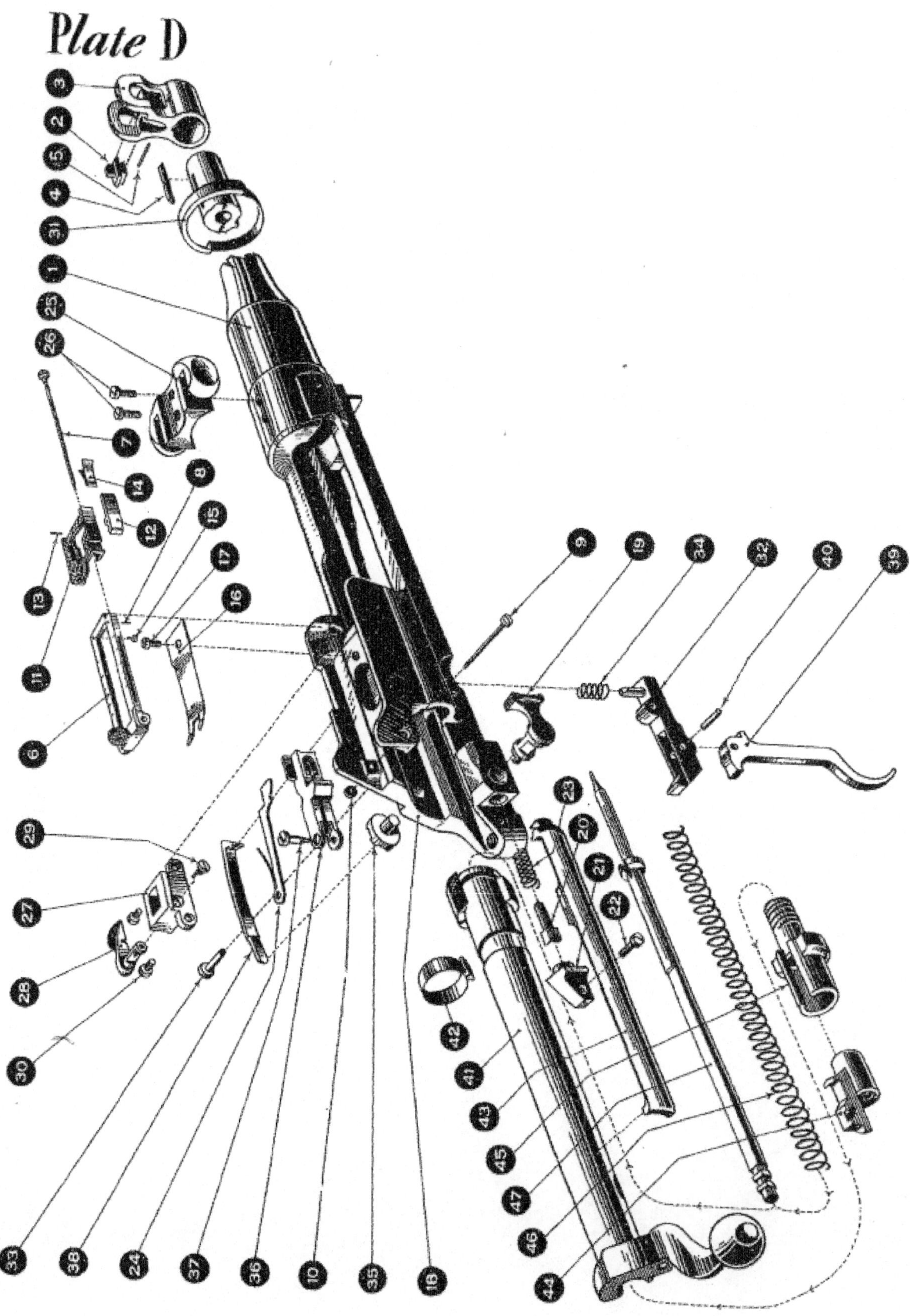
3
2
5
4
31
1
25
26
7
14
12
8
15
17
16
13
11
6
9
19
34
32
40
39
23
20
21
22
29
27
28
30
33
38
24
37
36
10
35
18
42
41
43
45
47
46
44

RIFLE No. 3, Mk.I*(T)

REF. NO.	DESIGNATION	VOCAB. NUMBER	MAT.	NO.OFF	REMARKS
. . .	RIFLE, NO.3. MK.I*(T), .303-in., pattern 1914 Ø	BA 0806 GA		1	NOTE:- THE DRAWING NUMBER FOR THIS RIFLE IS S.A.I.D.2058, 2059
. . .	BARREL ASSEMBLY	A		1	
D 1	BARREL		St.	1	
2	BLADE, foresight: Sizes:- .015"	BB 0810	St.	1	
	.0	" 0811			Ø Complete with SIGHT, TELESCOPIC and CASE, SIGHT, TELESCOPIC Vocab. No. (BA 0806)
	+ .015"	" 0812			
	.03"	" 0813			
	.045"	" 0814			
	.06"	" 0815			6. Complete with SLIDE; SCREW STOP; SCREW, FINE ADJUSTING, and PIN, RETAINING (BB 0839)
	.075"	" 0816			
	.09"	" 0817			
	.105"	" 0818			
	.12"				11. SLIDE, BACKSIGHT with CATCH and SPRING ASSEMBLED (BB 0889)
	.135"				
3	BLOCK, band, foresight		St.	1	
4	KEY		St.	1	
5	PIN, fixing		St.	1	
. . .	BODY, ASSEMBLY	A		1	
. . .	BACKSIGHT, No.3, ASSEMBLY	SA		1	
6	LEAF	BB 0839	St.	1	
7	SCREW, fine adjustment, .088" dia. x 36 T.P.I.	" 0878	St.	1	
8	PIN, retaining	" 0848	St.	1	
9	SCREW, axis, .096" dia. x 1.18" x 56 T.P.I.	" 0875	St.	1	
10	NUT	" 0840	St.	1	
11	SLIDE	" 0889	St.	1	
12	CATCH	" 0829	St.	1	
13	PIN, retaining	" 0847	St.	1	
14	SPRING	" 0892	St.	1	
15	SCREW, stop, .084" dia. x 57 T.P.I.	" 0885	St.	1	
16	SPRING	" 0896	St.	1	
17	SCREW, .144" dia. x .20" x 37 T.P.I.	" 0883	St.	1	

Plate D

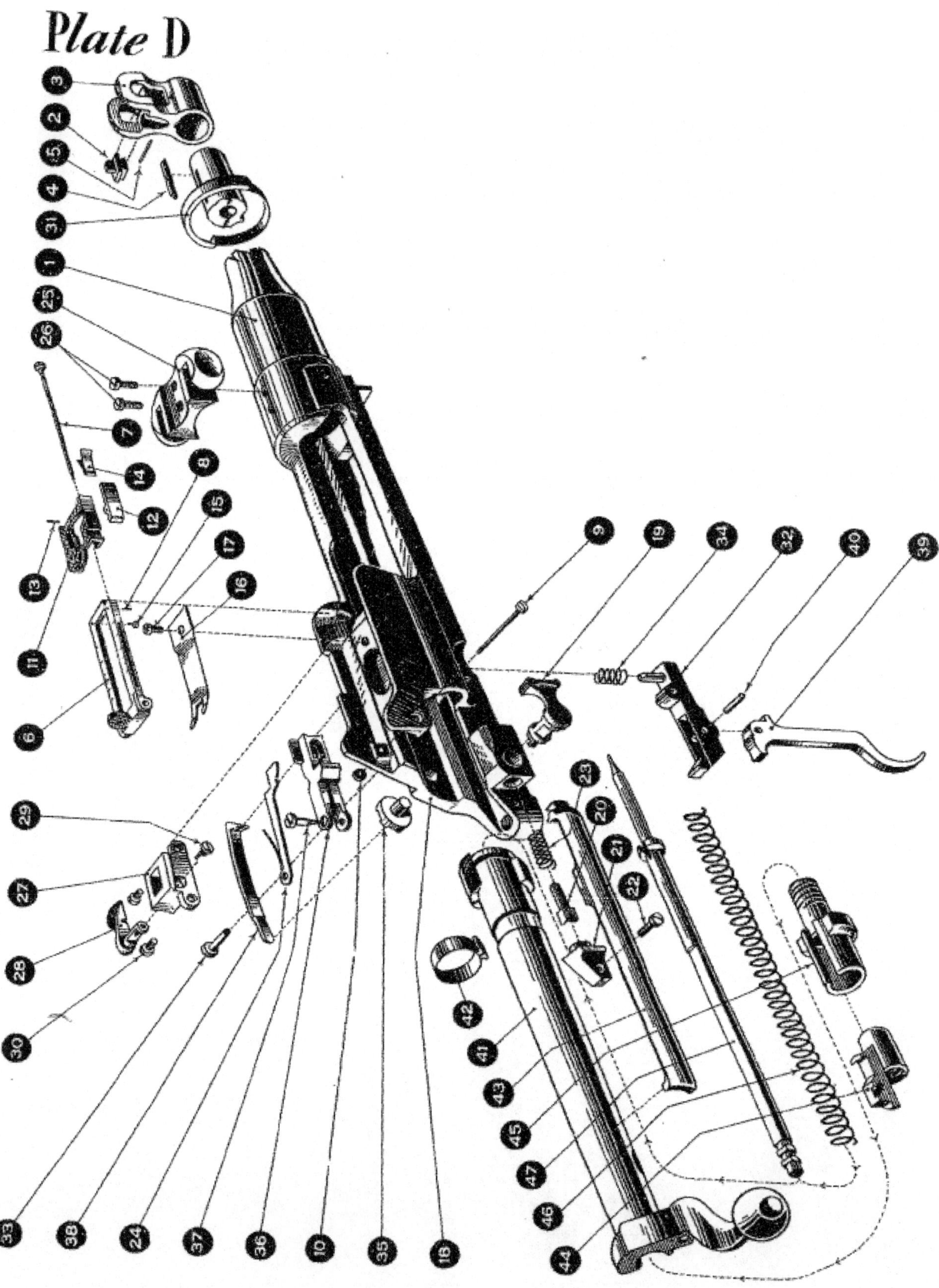
3
2
5
4
31
1
25
26
7
14
8
12
15
13
17
16
11
6
9
19
34
32
40
39
29
27
28
30
33
38
24
37
36
10
35
18
23
20
21
22
42
41
43
45
47
46
44

RIFLE No. 3, Mk.I*(T)

REF. NO.	DESIGNATION	VOCAB. NUMBER	MAT.	NO. OFF	REMARKS
. . .	RIFLE, NO.3 MK.I*(T), .303-in.,pattern 1914 (continued)				
. . .	BODY ASSEMBLY (continued)				
D 18	BODY		St.	1	
19	CATCH, safety, No.3	BB 0828	St.	1	
20	BOLT, locking	BB 0823	St.	1	
21	PLATE, cover	" 0860	St.	1	
22	SCREW, .12" dia. x 48 T.P.I.	" 0881	St.	1	
23	SPRING	" 0890	St.	1	
24	EJECTOR, No.3	" 0833	St.	1	
. . .	FITTINGS, TELESCOPE	SA		1	
25	FRONT		St.	1	
26	SCREW		St.	2	
27	REAR		St.	1	
28	CATCH		St.	1	
29	SCREW, retaining		St.	1	
30	SCREW		St.	2	
31	RING, guard, hand, No.3	BB 0874	St.	1	
32	SEAR, No.3	" 0887	St.	1	
33	PIN	" 0849	St.	1	
34	SPRING	" 0895	St.	1	
35	SIGHT, aperture, No.3 (stem removed)	" 0888	St.	1	
36	STOP, bolt, No.3	" 0910	St.	1	
37	SCREW, .126" dia. x 42 T.P.I.	" 0876	St.	1	
38	SPRING	" 0897	St.	1	
39	TRIGGER	" 0913	St.	1	
40	PIN, .1305" dia. x .33"	" 0852	St.	1	
. . .	BOLT, BREECH, NO.3, ASSEMBLY	A		1	
41	BOLT	BB 0822	St.	1	
42	RING, extractor	" 0873	St.	1	
43	EXTRACTOR	" 0834	St.	1	
44	PIECE, cocking	" 0830	St.	1	
45	PLUG	" 0872	St.	1	
46	SPRING, main	" 0893	St.	1	
47	STRIKER	" 0911	St.	1	

Plate E

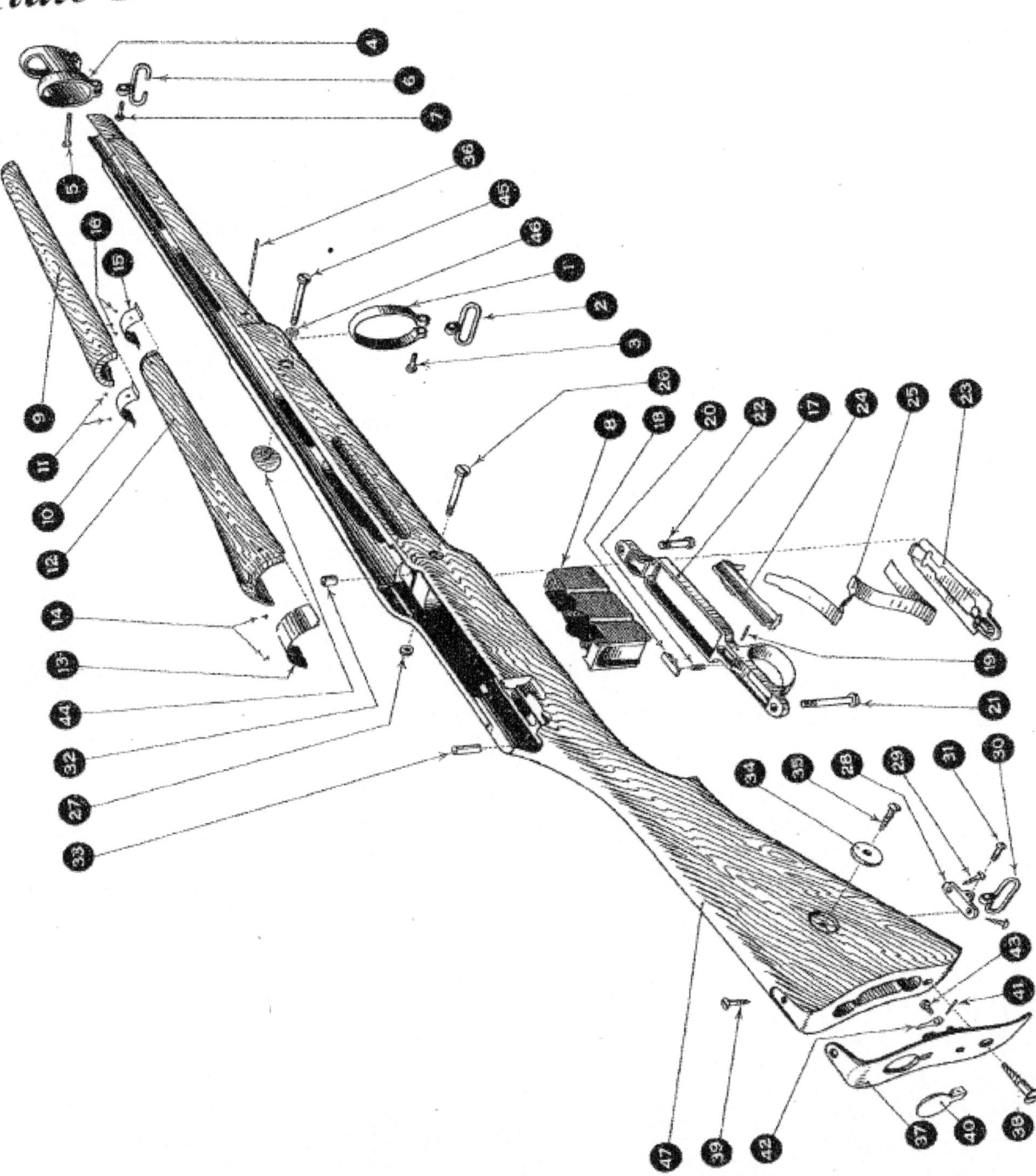
4
6
7
36
45
46
1
2
3
26
8
18
20
22
17
24
25
23
19
21
34
35
28
29
31
30
43
41
38
40
37
42
39
47
5
16
15
9
11
10
12
14
13
44
32
27
33

RIFLE No. 3, Mk.I*(T)

REF. NO.	DESIGNATION	VOCAB. NUMBER	MAT.	NO.OFF	REMARKS
. . .	RIFLE, NO. 3 MK.I*(T), .303-in., pattern 1914, (continued)				NOTE:- 9. GUARD HAND FRONT NO.3. BB 0836. complete with liner and rivets.
E 1	BAND, No.3	BB 0809	St.	1	
2	SWIVEL	" 0774	St.	(i)1	
3	SCREW, .1875" dia. x .53" x 33 T.P.I.	" 0744	St.	(i)1	12. GUARD HAND REAR NO.3. BB 0837, complete with 2 liners and rivets.
4	CAP, nose, No.3	" 0825	St.	1	
5	SCREW, .1656" dia. x 1.13" x 37 T.P.I.	" 0877	St.	1	
6	SWIVEL, piling, "A" or "B"	BB 0772 for"A" " 0773 " "B"	St.	1	17. GUARD, TRIGGER, NO.3. BB 0838, complete with catch,magazine, BB 0827; pin, BB 0846; spring, BB 0891.
7	SCREW, .1875" dia. x .53" x 33 T.P.I.	BB 0744	St.	(i)1	
8	CASE, magazine	" 0826	St.	1	
9	GUARD, hand, front, No.3	" 0836	Wood	1	
10	LINER		St.	1	
11	RIVET, .095" dia. x .156"		M.S.	2	
12	GUARD, hand, rear, No.3	" 0837	Wood	1	
13	LINER, back		St.	1	
14	RIVET, .095" dia. x .200"		M.S.	2	
15	LINER, front		St.	1	
16	RIVET, .095" dia. x .225"		M.S.	2	
17	GUARD, trigger, No.3	BB 0838	St.	1	
18	CATCH, magazine	" 0827	St.	1	
19	PIN	" 0846	St.	1	
20	SPRING	" 0891	St.	1	
21	SCREW, back, .25" dia. x .177" x 30 T.P.I.	" 0879	St.	1	
22	SCREW, front, .25" dia. x .92" x 30 T.P.I.	" 0880	St.	1	
23	PLATE, magazine	" 0862	St.	1	
24	PLATFORM, magazine	" 0867	St.	1	
25	SPRING, magazine	" 0894	St.	1	

Plate E

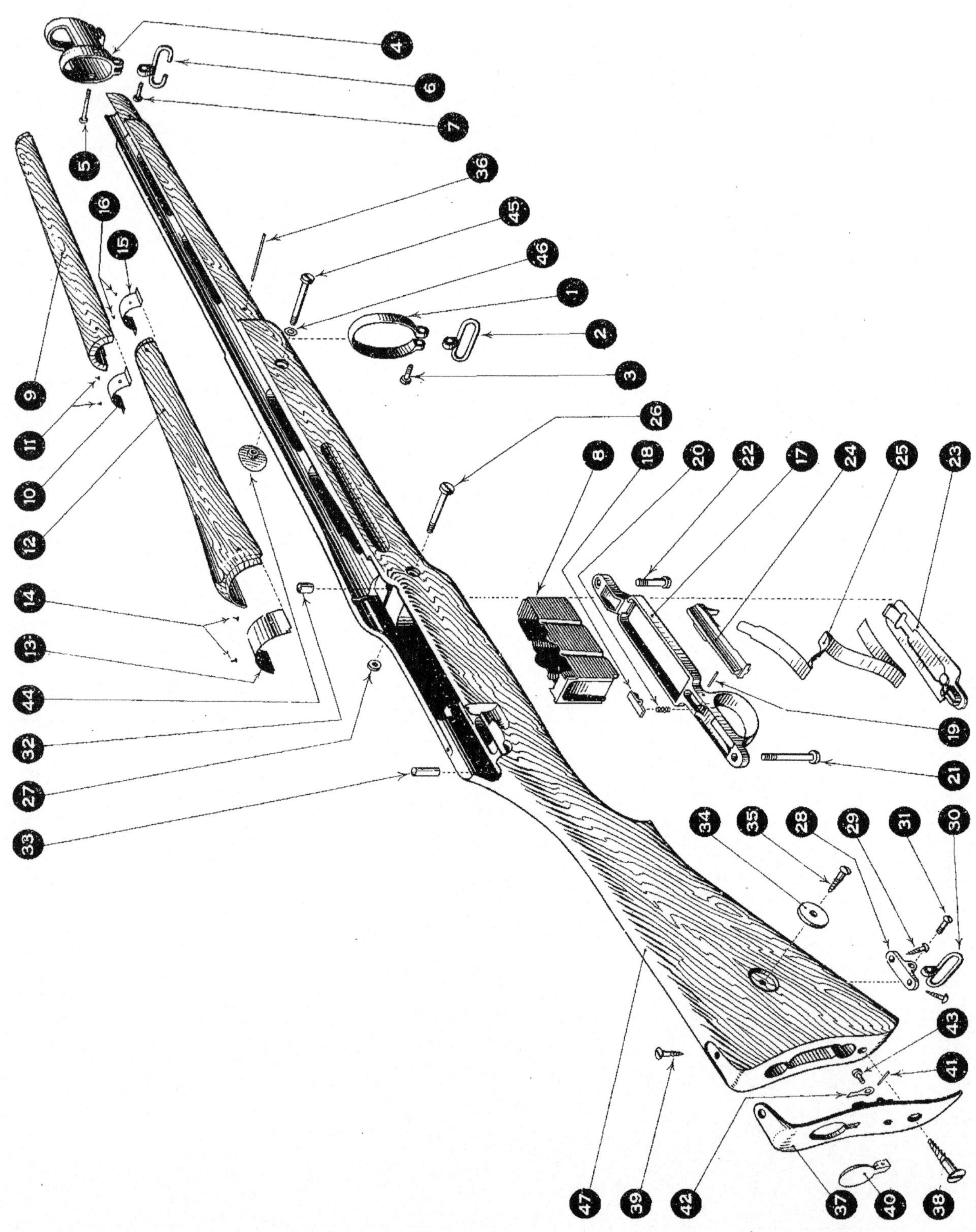
4
6
7
5
36
45
46
1
2
3
26
16
15
9
11
10
12
14
13
44
32
27
33
8
18
20
22
17
24
25
23
19
21
34
35
28
29
31
30
43
41
47
39
42
37
40
38

RIFLE No. 3, Mk.I*(T)

REF. NO.	DESIGNATION	VOCAB. NUMBER	MAT.	NO. OFF	REMARKS
. . .	RIFLE, NO.3 MK.I*(T), .303-in., pattern 1914 (continued)				NOTE:-
. . .	STOCK ASSEMBLY	A		1	Ø DISC, marking, brass, sandblasted BB 0677.
26	BOLT, tie, No.3, .1875" dia. x 33 T.P.I.	BB 0814	St.	1	DISC, marking, brass, polished BB 0678.
[illegible]	NUT	" 0841	St.	1	
28	BRACKET, butt	" 0664	St.	1	
29	SCREW, .198" dia. x .905" x 10 T.P.I.	" 0725	St.	(i)2	37. PLATE BUTT, NO.3. BB 0861; issued with trap and spring assembled.
30	SWIVEL	" 0774	St.	(i)1	
31	SCREW, .1875" dia. x .53" x 33 T.P.I.	" 0744	St.	(i)1	
32	COLLAR, front, No.3	" 0831	St.	1	
33	COLLAR, rear, No.3	" 0832	St.	1	47. STOCK NO.3. BB 0909; issued with band, stop pin complete.
34	DISC, marking, brass	Ø	Br.	1	
35	SCREW, brass, .186" dia. x .715" x 12 T.P.I.	BB 0731	Br.	1	
	or				
34	DISC, marking, steel.	BB 0679	St.	1	
35	SCREW, steel, .186" dia. x .715" x 12 T.P.I.		St.	1	
36	PIN, stop, band, .10" dia. x 1.34" long	BB 0830	St.	1	
37	PLATE, butt, No.3	" 0861	St.	1	
38	SCREW, .31" dia. x 1.412" x 8 T.P.I.	" 0882	St.	1	
39	SCREW, strap, .2" dia. x .87" x 10 T.P.I.	" 0886	St.	1	
40	TRAP	" 0912	St.	1	
41	PIN, .104" dia. x .8" long	" 0851	St.	1	
42	SPRING	" 0898	St.	1	
43	SCREW, .1656" dia. x .361" x 37 T.P.I.	" 0884	St.	1	
44	PLATE, sight, dial		St.	1	
45	SCREW, fixing, .1656" dia. x 1.15" x 37 T.P.I.		St.	1	
46	WASHER, .375" dia. x .018" thick		St.	1	
47	STOCK, No.3	BB 0909	Wood	1	

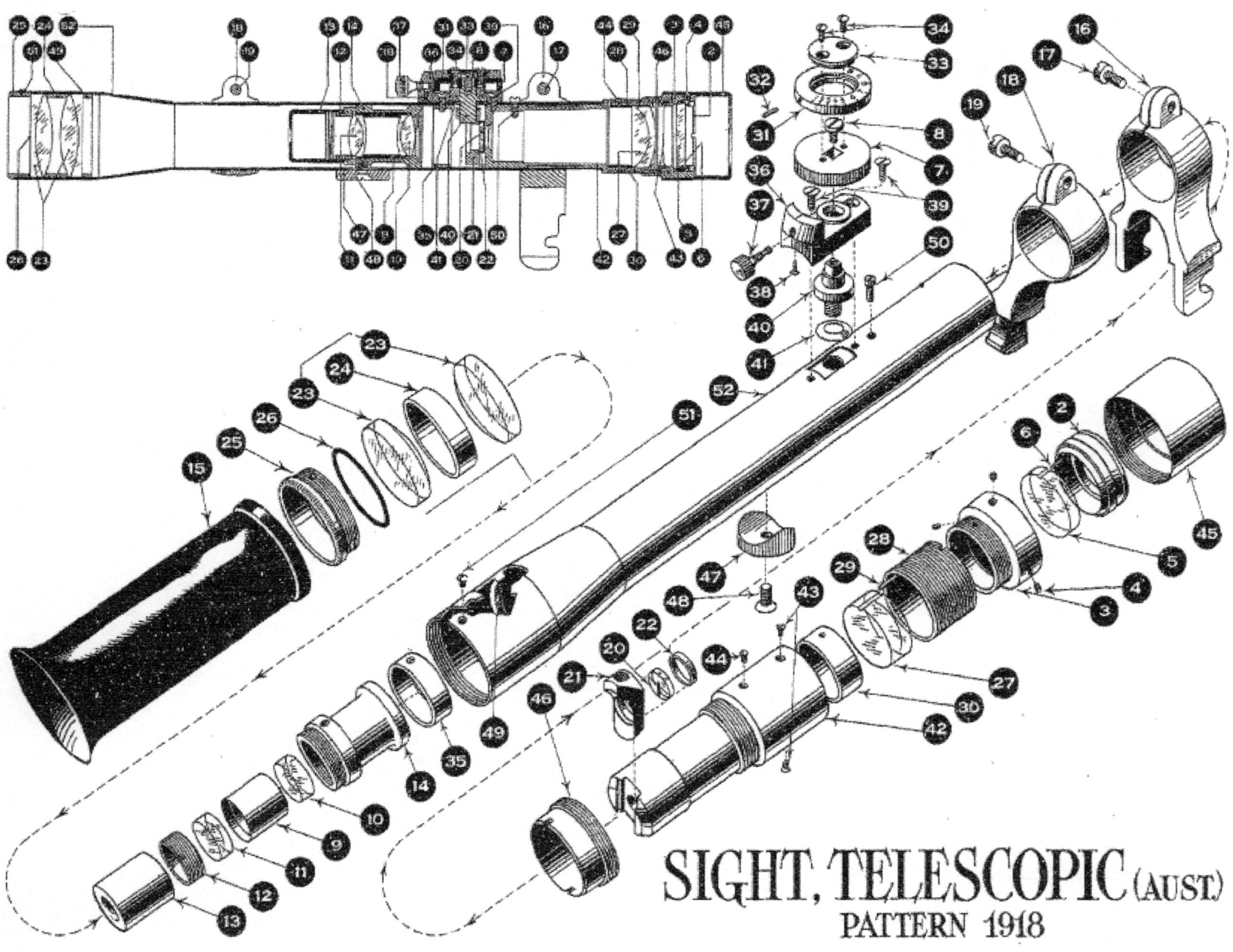
SIGHT, TELESCOPIC (AUST.)
PATTERN 1918

RIFLE No. 3, Mk.I*(T)

[illegible] NO.	DESIGNATION	VOCAB. NUMBER	MAT.	NO.OFF	DRAWING NUMBER	
. . .	SIGHT, TELESCOPIC, PATT.1918 (AUST.)/1	BAA. 3600 GA		1	ADD(A)57-100	
F 1	CASE (Illustrated on Key Plate)	BA. 0066	Pl.	1		
2	CELL, prism	BAA. 3601	Br.	1	" 57-114	
3	ADAPTER	BAA. 3601	Br.	1	" 57-115	
4	SCREW, fixing, 8 BA x .100"	BAA. 3603	M.S.	2	" 57-116	
5	WINDOW	BAA. 3604	Gl.	1	" 57-112	
6	WIRE, .016" dia. x .093"		Br.	1	" 57-114	
7	DRUM, range	BAA. 3606	Br.	1	" 57-130	
8	SCREW, fixing	BAA. 3607	M.S.	1	" 57-125	
. . .	ERECTOR, ASSEMBLY	BAA. 3608 A		1	" 57-105	
9	CELL, erecting lenses	BAA. 3609	Br.	1	" 57-108	
10	LENS, No.2	BAA. 3610	Gl.	1	" 57-107	
11	LENS, No.3	BAA. 3611	Gl.	1	" 57-109	
12	RING, clamp	BAA. 3612	Br.	1	" 57-110	
13	RING, locking, stoplight	BAA. 3613	Br.	1	" 57-111	
14	TUBE	BAA. 3614	Br.	1	" 57-106	
15	EYEGUARD, detachable	BAA. 3615	Ru.	1	ADD(A)45-109	
16	FITTINGS, overhead, front	BAA. 3616	M.S.	1	ADD(A)57-123	
17	SCREW, clamping	BAA. 3617	M.S.	(1)1	" 57-124	
18	FITTINGS, overhead, rear	BAA. 3618	M.S.	1	" 57-137	
19	SCREW, clamping	BAA. 3617	M.S.	(1)1	" 57-124	
. . .	GRATICULE ASSEMBLY	BAA. 3619 A		1	" 57-101	
20	GRATICULE	BAA. 3620	Gl.	1	" 57-103	
21	GUIDE	BAA. 3621	Br.	1	" 57-104	
22	RING	BAA. 3622	Br.	1	" 57-102	
23	LENS, eye, No.4 & No.5	BAA. 3623	Gl.	2	" 57-139	
24	RING, distance	BAA. 3624	Br.	1	" 57-140	
25	RING, locking	BAA. 3625	Br.	1	" 57-141	
26	RING, sealing	BAA. 3688	Fi.	1		

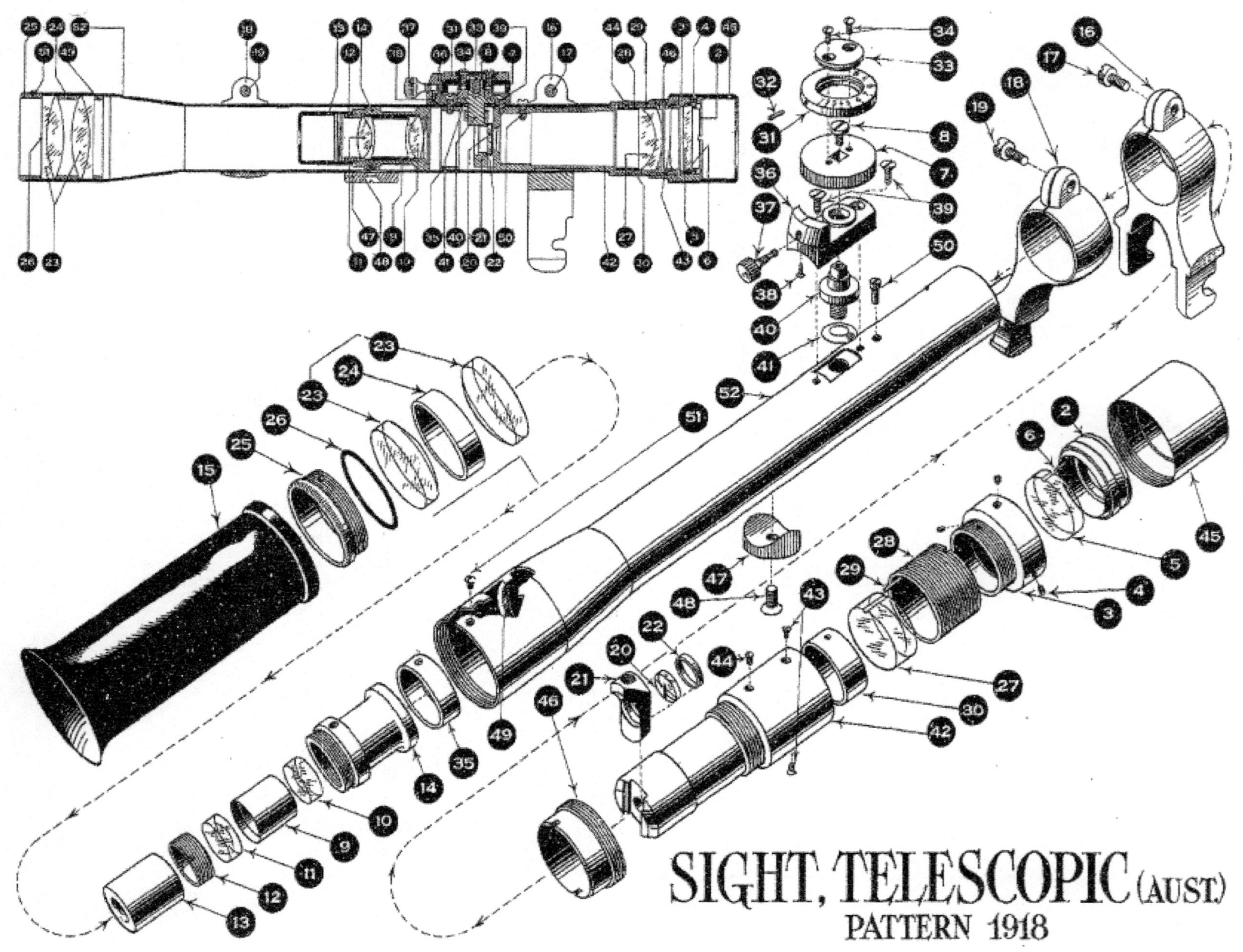
SIGHT, TELESCOPIC (AUST.)
PATTERN 1918

RIFLE No. 3, Mk.I*(T)

REF. NO.	DESIGNATION	VOCAB. NUMBER	MAT.	NO. OFF	DRAWING NUMBER	REMARKS
. . .	SIGHT, TELESCOPIC, PATT. 1918 (AUST.)/1	BAA.3600 GA		1	ADD(A)57-100	
F 27	OBJECT-GLASS (lens No.1)	BAA.3626	Gl.	1	" 57-119	
28	CELL	BAA.3627	Br.	1	" 57-118	
29	WIRE, .016" dia. x .187"		Br.	1	" 57-118	
30	RING, burnishing	BAA.3629	Br.	1	" 57-120	
31	RING, scale, range	BAA.3630	Br.	1	" 57-128	
32	PIN, .042" dia. x .133"	BAA.3631	Br.	1	" 57-128	
33	WASHER, holding	BAA.3632	Br.	1	" 57-126	
34	SCREW, inst. hd., 8 BA x 1/2"	VPA.3600	M.S.	2	" 57-100/5	* Shorten to .187"
35	RING, stiffening	BAA.3634	Br.	1	" 57-134	
36	SADDLE	BAA.3635	Br.	1	" 57-129	
37	SCREW, clamping, range drum	BAA.3636	M.S.	1	" 57-132	
38	SCREW, stop	BAA.3637	M.S.	1	" 57-133	
39	SCREW, c'sk.hd., 6 BA x 3/8"	G1/GAA.6097	M.S.	2	" 57-100/4	Sh.rten to .234"
40	SCREW, elevating	BAA.3638	M.S.	1	" 57-127	
41	WASHER, spring	BAA.3639	S.S.	1	" 57-131	
42	SLEEVE, connecting	BAA.3640	Br.	1	" 57-122	
43	SCREW, c'sk.hd., 8 BA x 3/8"	G1/GAA.6099	M.S.	2	" 57-100/1	Shorten to .093"
44	SCREW, I.H., 10 BA x 1/2"	VPA.3601	M.S.	1	" 57-100/2	Shorten to .109"
45	SHADE, ray	BAA.3641	Br.	1	" 57-113	
46	COLLAR, fixing	BAA.3642	Br.	1	" 57-117	
47	SLIDE, focussing	BAA.3643	Br.	1	" 57-135	
48	SCREW, clamping	BAA.3644	M.S.	1	" 57-136	
. . .	TUBE, BODY, ASSEMBLY	BAA.3645 A		1	" 57-121	
49	RING, positioning, lens, eye	BAA.3646	Br.	1	" 57-138	
50	SCREW, ch.hd., 6 BA x 1/2"	G1/GAA.3779	M.S.	1	" 57-100/3	Shorten to .200"
51	SCREW, inst. hd., 10 BA x 1/2"	VPA.3601	M.S.	1	" 57-100/6	Shorten to .078"
52	TUBE	BAA.3647	M.S.	1	" 57-121	

Plate G

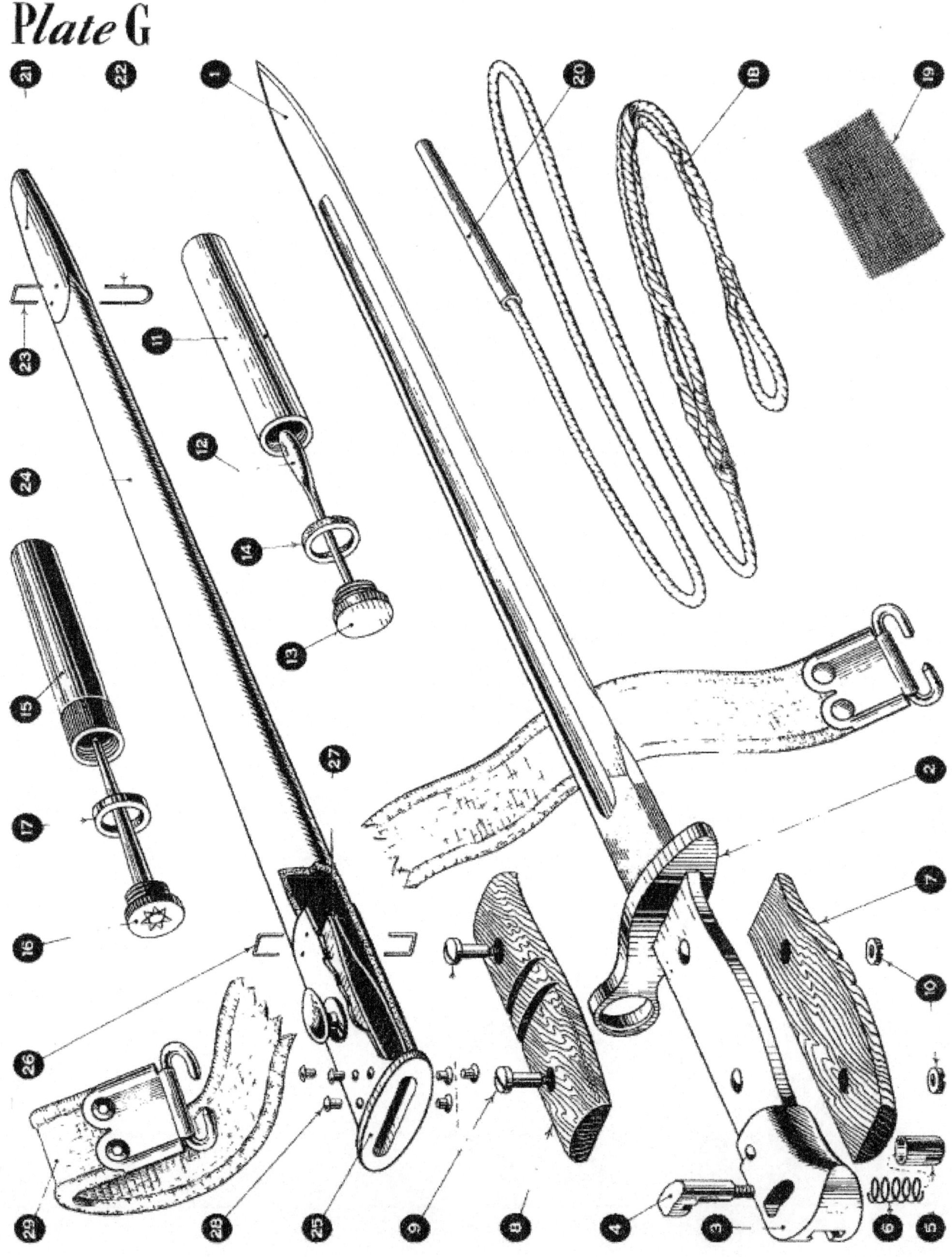

REF. NO.	DESIGNATION	VOCAB. NUMBER	MAT.	NO.OFF	DRAWING NUMBER	REMARKS
. . .	ACCESSORIES, RIFLE NO.3, MK.I*(T), pattern 1918					NOTE:-
. . .	BAYONET, No.3, Mk.I	BA 0030 A		1	S.A.I.D.2474	/Ø Pull-through, single, Mk.IV. "A" BA 0517
G 1	BLADE		St.	1		Pull-through, single, Mk.IV. "B" BA 0518
2	CROSSPIECE brazed to blade		St.	1		
3	POMMEL		St.	1		
4	BOLT	BB 0031	St.	1		
5	NUT	" 0033	St.	1		
6	SPRING	" 0036	St.	1		
7	GRIP, left PAIR	" 0032	Wood	1		
8	GRIP, right	" 0032	Wood	1		
9	SCREW, grip	" 0035	St.	2		
10	NUT	" 0034	St.	2		
. . .	BOTTLE, OIL, MK.IV.	BA 0053 A		1		
11	BODY		Br.	1		
12	SPOON	BB 0054	St.	1		
13	STOPPER	" 0055	Br.	1		
14	WASHER	" 0056	L.	1		
	or					
. . .	BOTTLE, OIL, MK.V.	A		1	DD(E)2562	
15	BODY		P.M.	1		
16	STOPPER, with rod		P.M.	1		
17	WASHER		L.	1		
. . .	PULL-THROUGH, single, Mk.IV. "A" or "B"	Ø		1	S.A.I.D.257 E	
18	CORD, 30"	BB 0520	Cord	1		
19	GAUZE (Not provided with "B" pull-throughs)	" 0521	St.	1		
20	WEIGHT	" 0522	Br.	1		
. . .	SCABBARD, BAYONET, NO.1, MK.II.	BA 1211 A		1	S.A.I.D.2474	
21	CHAPE	BB 1212	St.	1		
22	LACE, long, .056" dia. x 1.35", wire	" 1213	M.S.	1		
23	LACE, short, .056" dia. x 1.05", wire	" 1214	M.S.	(i)1		
24	LEATHER, finished	" 8353B	L.	1		
25	LOCKET	" 1216	St.	1		
26	LACE, short, .056" dia. x 1.05", wire	" 1214	M.S.	(i)2		
27	SPRING		St.	2		
28	RIVET		M.S.	6		
29	SLING, rifle, web. (complete)	AA 1657	Web.	1		

Key Plate

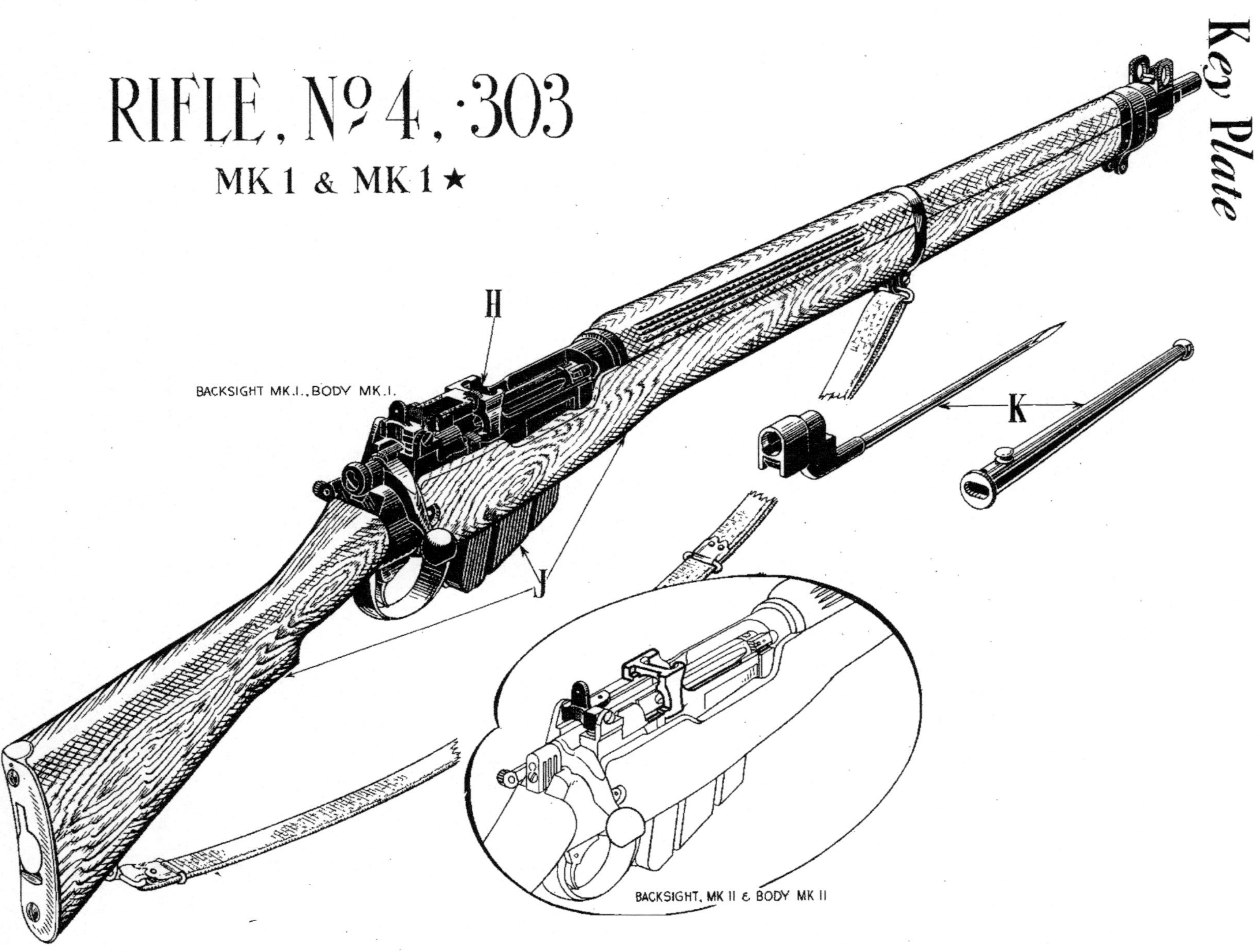
RIFLE, No 4, ·303
MK 1 & MK 1★
H
BACKSIGHT MK.I., BODY MK.I.
K
J
BACKSIGHT, MK II & BODY MK II

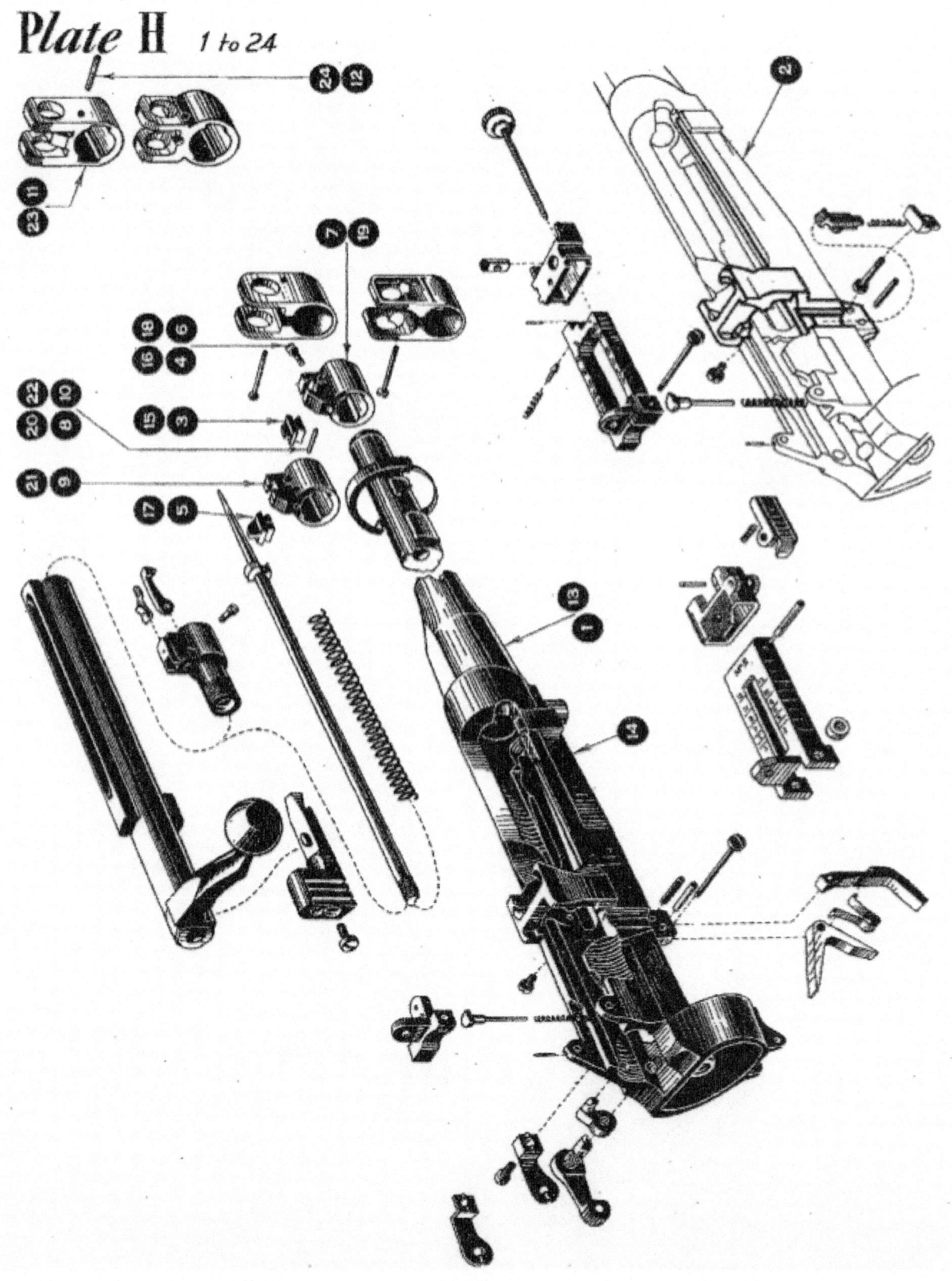
Plate II 1 to 24
24 12
23 11
7 19
18 6
16 4
22 10
20 8
15 3
21 9
17 5
2
13 1
14

RIFLE No. 4, Mk.I and Mk.I*

REF NO.	DESIGNATION	VOCAB. NO.	KAT.	NO. OFF	DRAWING NO.	[illegible]
...	RIFLE,NO.4,MK.I & MK.I*,.303-IN.					
...	BARREL WITH BODY, ASSEMBLY					For Mk.I Rifle
...	MK.I	NB 8556		1	DD(E)450/3	With 5-groove rifling
...	MK.II ... ... *	" 8681		1	" " /110	With 2-groove rifling
...	MK.III	" 8682		1	" " /119	Fabricated
X 1	BARREL,MK.I (c)	" 8557	St.	1	" " /3	With 5-groove rifling
...	BARREL,MK.II (c)	" 8683	St.	1	" " /110	With 2-groove rifling
...	BARREL,Mk.III. (c)	" 8684	St.	1	" " /119	Fabricated
2	BODY,Mk.I.		St.	1	" " /6R	
...	FORESIGHT					
3	BLADE,"O",Mk.I ... ... *	" 8562	St.	1	" " /4C	
4	SCREW ... ... *	" 8033	St.	1	" " /56	Used with Block, band, foresight, Mk.I. only
5	or BLADE,"O",MK.I*	" 8687	St.	1	" " /97	
6	SCREW ... ... *	" 8033	St.	1	" " /56	Used with Block, band, foresight, Mk.I. only
7	BLOCK,band,Mk.I.		St.	1	" " /5	
8	PIN		St.	1	" " /35	
9	or BLOCK,band,Mk.II.		St.	1	" " /96	
10	PIN		St.	1	" " /35	
11	or BRACKET		St.	1	" " /120	
12	PIN		St.	1	" " /105	
...	BARREL,WITH MK.II.BODY,ASSEMBLY ...					For Mk.I* Rifle
...	MK.I.	" 8556		1	" " /3	With 5-groove rifling
...	MK.II.	" 8681		1	" " /110	With 2-groove rifling
...	MK.III.	" 8682		1	" " /119	Fabricated
13	BARREL,MK.I (c)	" 8557	St.	1	" " /3	With 5-groove rifling
...	BARREL,MK.II (c)	" 8683	St.	1	" " /110	With 2-groove rifling
...	BARREL,MK.III (c)	" 8684	St.	1	" " /119	Fabricated
14	BODY,MK.II.	" 8658	St.	1	DD(E)2838/1	
...	FORESIGHT					
15	BLADE,"O",MK.I ... ... *	" 8562	St.	1	DD(E)450/4C	Used with Block, band, foresight, Mk.I only
16	SCREW ... ... *	" 8033	St.	1	" " /56	
17	or BLADE,"O",MK.I*	" 8687	St.	1	" " /97	
18	SCREW ... ... *	" 8033	St.	1	" " /56	Used with Block, band, foresight, Mk.I only
19	BLOCK,band,Mk.I		St.	1	" " /5	
20	PIN		St.	1	" " /35	
21	or BLOCK,band,Mk.II		St.	1	" " /96	
22	PIN		St.	1	" " /35	
23	or BRACKET		St.	1	" " /120	
24	PIN		St.	1	" " /105	

(c) Barrels not issued separately.

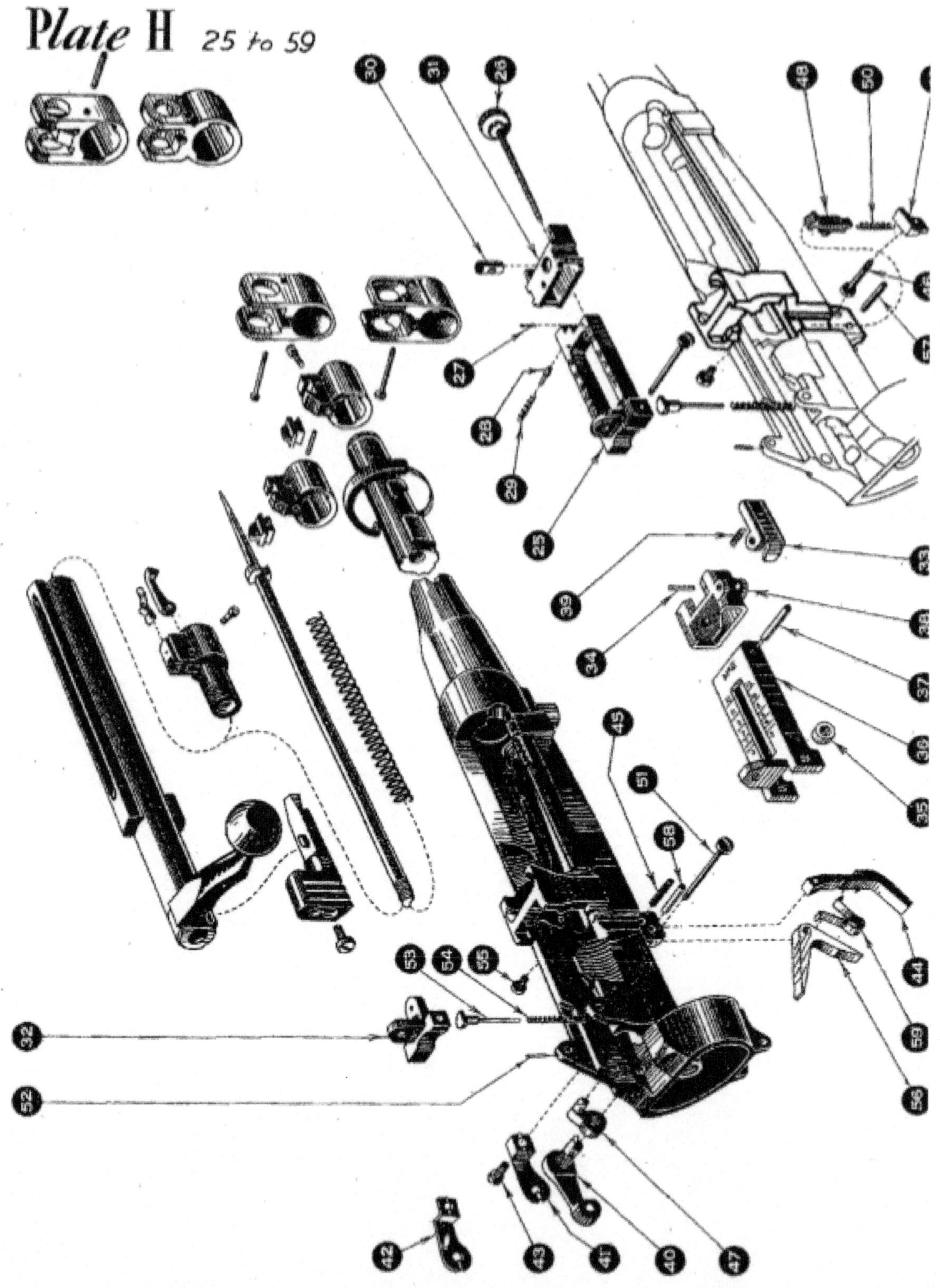
Plate II 25 to 59

RIFLE No. 4, Mk.I and Mk.I*

DIAG. NO.	DESIGNATION		VOCAB. NO.	MAT.	NO. OFF	DRAWING NO.	REMARKS
...	RIFLE,NO.4,MK.I.& MK.I*,.303-IN. (contd.)						
...	BACKSIGHT,MK.I ASSEMBLY	*	BB 8023		1	DD(E)450/A	
H25	LEAF	*	" 8589	St.	1	" " /28R	For Backsight, Mk.I.
26	SCREW,adjusting		" 8604	St.	1	" " /55	
27	PIN,retaining		" 8032	St.	1	" " /36	
28	PLUNGER		" 8599	St.	1	" " /47	
29	SPRING		" 8626	S.S.	1	" " /70	
30	NUT		" 8590	St.	1	" " /30R	
31	SLIDE	*	" 8620	St.	1	" " /67R	For Backsight, Mk.I.
32	BACKSIGHT,MK.II.	*	" 8662		1	" " /109	300-yds. and 600-yds.
...	BACKSIGHT,MK.III ASSEMBLY	*	" 8673		1	" " /X	
33	CATCH	*	" 8674	St.	1	" " /98	
34	PIN	*	" 8677	St.	1	" " /101	
35	COLLAR	*	" 8675	St.	1	" " /99	For Backsight, Mk.III.
36	LEAF,Mk.II.	*	" 8676	St.	1	" " /100	For Backsight, Mk.III.
37	PIN,stop	*	" 8678	St.	1	" " /102	
38	SLIDE,Mk.II,Assd.	*	" 8679		1	" " /103	For Backsights Mk.III with catch & spring Assd.
39	SPRING,catch	*	" 8680	S.S.	1	" " /104	
40	BOLT,locking	*	" 8026	St.	1	" " /8	
41	SPRING	*	" 8040	S.S.	1	" " /77	Sheet 1
42	SPRING			S.S.	1	" " /77	Alt. Patt. Sheet 2
43	SCREW	*	" 8614	St.	1	" " /64	Also for Spring, trap, butt plate
44	CATCH,magazine	*	" 8575	St.	1	" " /15	
45	PIN	*	" 8669	St.	1	DD(E)2838/3	For Mk.I* rifle. To be demanded as Pin,sear,Mk.II.
46	SCREW		" 8606	St.	1	DD(E)450/49	For Mk.I rifle
47	CATCH,safety	*	" 8576	St.	1	" " /17	
48	CATCH,head,breech,bolt		" 8574	St.	1	" " /16	For Mk.I rifle
49	PLATE		" 8596	St.	1	" " /41A	For Mk.I rifle
50	SPRING		" 8623	S.S.	1	" " /71	For Mk.I rifle
51	PIN,axis,backsight	*	" 8030	St.	1	" " /32A	
52	PIN,retaining	*	" 8031	St.	1	" " /27	
53	PLUNGER,backsight	*	" 8598	St.	1	" " /50R	
54	SPRING	*	" 8625	S.S.	1	" " /69R	
55	SCREW,ejector	*	" 8035	St.	1	" " /53	
56	SEAR	*	" 8618	St.	1	" " /66	
57	PIN,Mk.I.	*	" 8591	St.	1	" " /38	For Mk.I rifle. Also for Pin, trigger
58	PIN,Mk.II.	*	" 8669	St.	1	DD(E)2838/3	For Mk.I* rifle
59	SPRING	*	" 8627	St.	1	DD(E)450/76	Rifles No.1 - Spring, sear may also be used

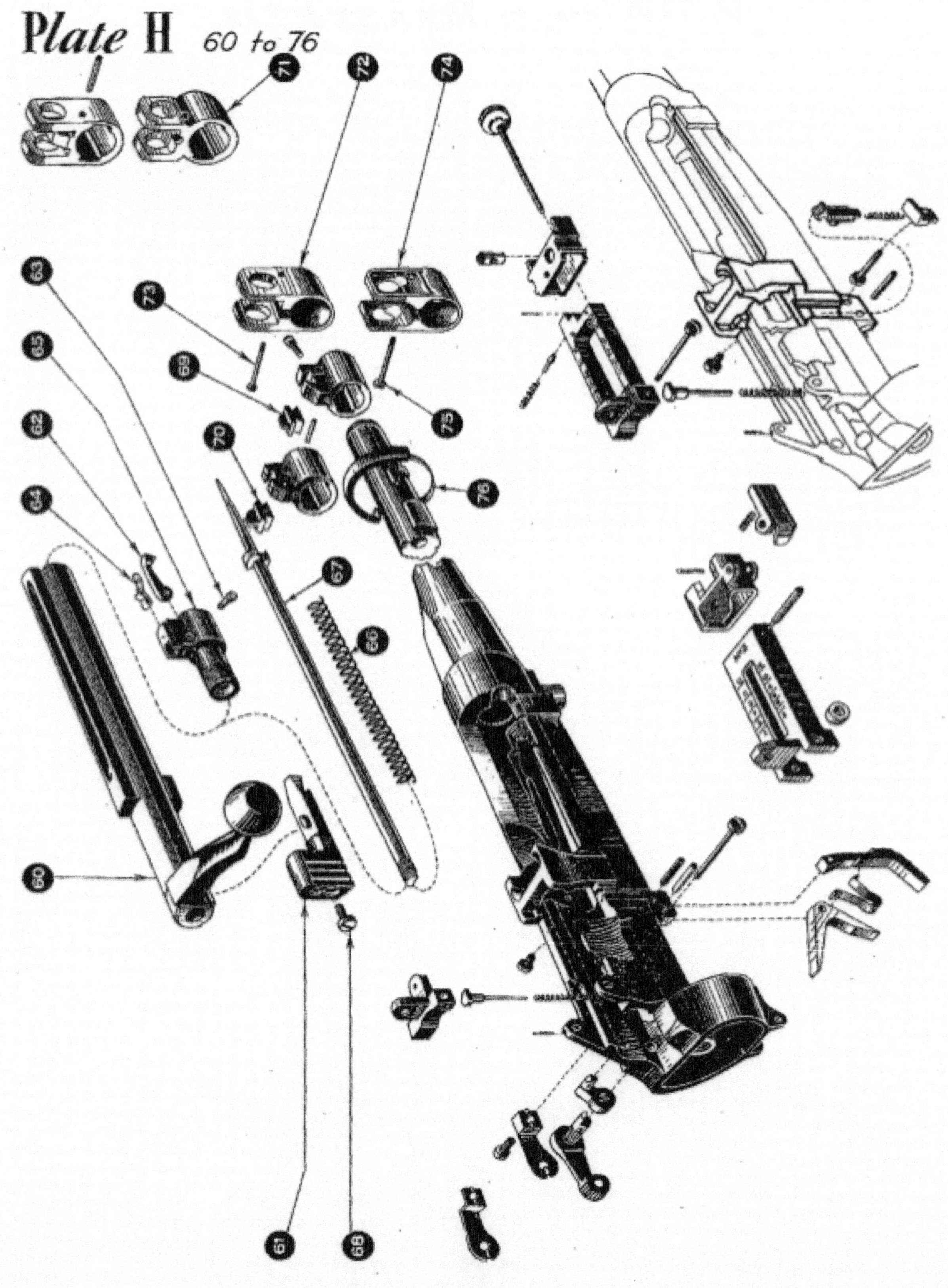
Plate H 60 to 76
71
72
74
63
73
65
69
62
70
75
76
64
67
66
60
61
68

RIFLE No. 4, Mk.I and Mk.I*

REF. NO.	DESIGNATION		VOCAB. NO.	MAT.	NO. OFF	DRAWING NO.	REMARKS
...	RIFLE, NO.4, MK.I & MK.I*, .303-IN. (contd.)						
...	BOLT, BREECH, ASSEMBLY					DD(E)430/C	
H60	BOLT	*	BB 8566	St.	1	" " /7	
61	COCKING-PIECE, Mk.II.	*	" 8650	St.	1	" " /18B	
62	EXTRACTOR	*	" 8028	St.	1	" " /22	
63	SCREW	*	" 8608	St.	1	" " /54	
64	SPRING...	*	" 8041	S.S.	1	" " /72A	
65	HEAD						(d) Number "O" to 3 increase in length by increments of 0.003-in.
...	No."O" (d)	*	" 8584	St.	1	" " /26	
...	No.1 (d)	*	" 8585	St.	1	" " /26	
...	No.2 (d)	*	" 8586	St.	1	" " /26	
...	No.3 (d)	*	" 8587	St.	1	" " /26	
66	SPRING, main	*		S.S.	1	" " /71	To be demanded under Rifles No.1 (Cat.No. BB 0754)
67	STRIKER	*	" 8634	St.	1	" " /79A	
68	SCREW	*	" 8616	St.	1	" " /60B	
...	FORESIGHT						
69	BLADE, Mk.I.					" " /4C	Used with Block, band, foresight, Mk.I.
...	- .03-in.	*	" 8560	St.	1	" " /4C	
...	- .015-in.	*	" 8561	St.	1	" " /4C	
...	"O"	*	" 8562	St.	1	" " /4C	
...	+ .015-in.	*	" 8563	St.	1	" " /4C	
..	+ .030-in.	*	" 8564	St.	1	" " /4C	
..	+ .045-in.	*	" 8565	St.	1	" " /4C	
..	+ .06-in.	*	" 8666	St.	1	" " /4C	
..	+ .075-in.	*	" 8667	St.	1	" " /4C	
70	BLADE, Mk.I*					" " /97	Used with Block, band, foresight, Mk.II.
..	- .03-in.		" 8685	St.	1	" " /97	
..	- .015-in.		" 8686	St.	1	" " /97	
..	"O"		" 8687	St.	1	" " /97	
..	+ .015-in.		" 8688	St.	1	" " /97	
..	+ .03-in.		" 8689	St.	1	" " /97	
..	+ .045-in.		" 8690	St.	1	" " /97	
..	+ .06-in.		" 8691	St.	1	" " /97	
..	+ .075-in.		" 8692	St.	1	" " /97	
71	PROTECTOR, Mk.I	*	" 8600	St.	1	" " /39	Sheet 1
72	PROTECTOR, Mk.I			St.	1	" " /39	Alt. Patt. Sheet 2
73	SCREW, Mk.I	*	" 8036	St.	1	" " /62A	
74	or PROTECTOR, Mk.II		" 8693	St.	1	" " /95	
75	SCREW, Mk.II		" 8610	St.	1	" " /58	Also for screw, guard, trigger, back
76	RING, retaining, rear, handguard ...	*	" 8602	St.	1	" " /45	

Plate J

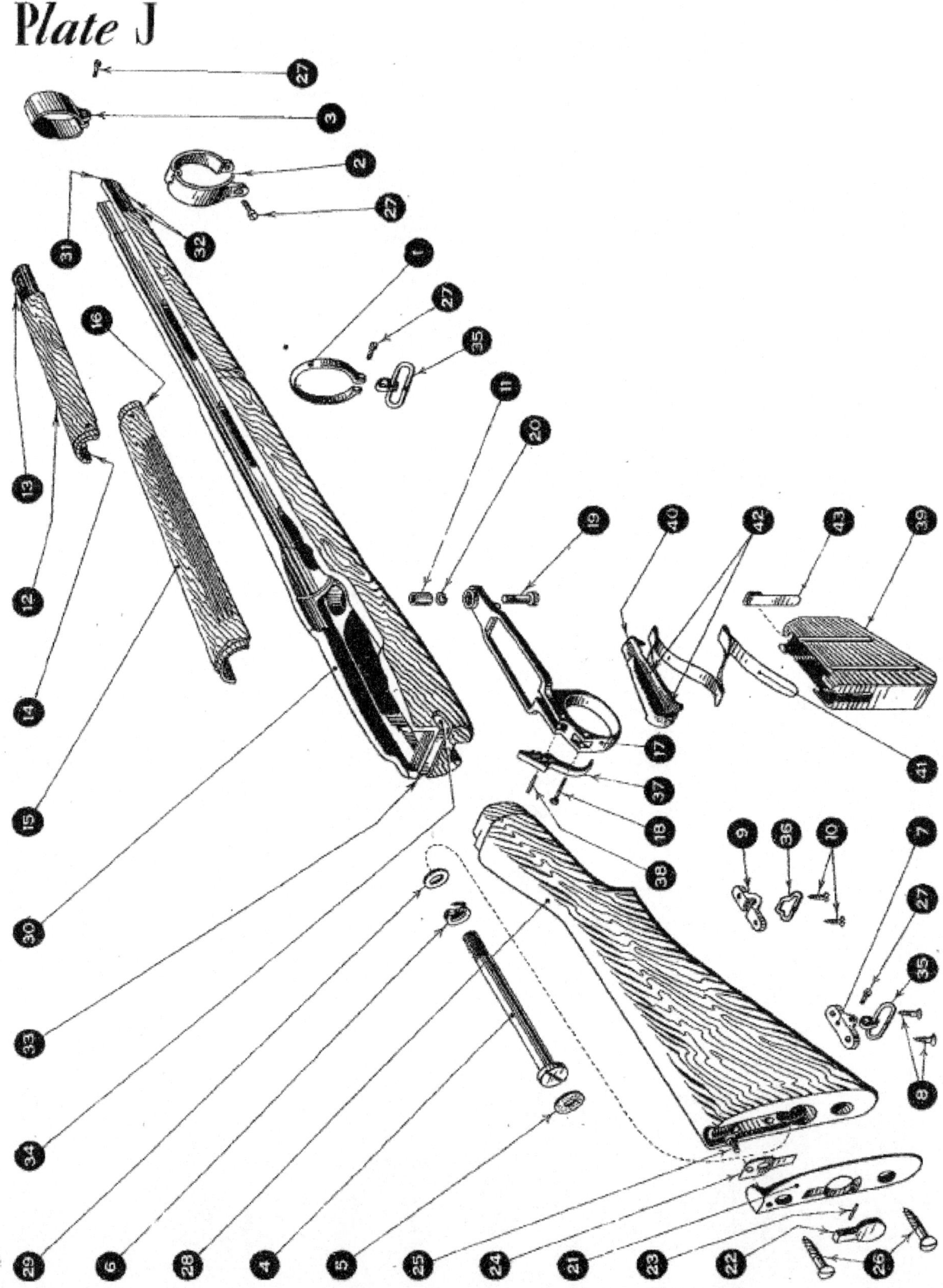

27
3
2
27
31
32
1
27
35
11
20
16
13
12
14
15
30
19
40
42
43
39
17
37
18
38
41
9
36
10
7
27
35
8
33
34
29
6
28
4
5
25
24
21
23
22
26

RIFLE No. 4, Mk.I and Mk.I*

REF. NO.	DESIGNATION		VOCAB. NO.	MAT.	NO. OFF	DRAWING NO.	REMARKS
...	RIFLE,NO.4,MK.I & MK.I*,.303-IN. (contd.)						
J 1	BAND,lower...	*	BB 8554	St.	1	DD(E)450/2	
2	BAND,upper...	*	" 8555	St.	1	"" " /91A	Hinged type
3	BAND,upper...	*	" 8555	St.	1	" " /91A	Solid type. Sheet 2 & 3 alt.
4	BOLT,stock...	*	" 8567	St.	1	" " /9	
5	WAD	*		L.	1	" " /86	To be demanded under Rifles No.1 (Cat.No. 0777)
6	WASHER,spring	*	" 8641	S.S.	1	" " /90	
7	BRACKET,Mk.I.	*		St.	1	" " /10	For Butt swivel to be demanded under Rifles No.1 (Cat.No. BB 0664) used with Swivel, sling, Mk.I.
8	SCREW	*	" 8605	St.	2	" " /48	
9	BRACKET,Mk.II.	*	" 8672	St.	1	" " /93	For Butt swivel used with Swivel, sling, Mk.II.
10	SCREW	*	" 8605	St.	2	" " /48	
11	COLLAR	*	" 8579	St.	1	" " /19	For Trigger guard screw
12	GUARD,band,front,Assd.	*	" 8580		1	" " /D	
13	CAP			St.	1	" " /12B	
14	LINER				1	" " /29	
15	GUARD,band,rear,Assd.	*	" 8581		1	" " /E	
16	LINER				1	" " /29	
17	GUARD,trigger	*	" 8582	St.	1	" " /25	
18	SCREW,back	*	" 8610	St.	1	" " /58	Also for Protector, foresight, Mk.II.
19	SCREW,front	*	" 8611	St.	1	" " /59	
20	WASHER...	*	" 8640	St.	1	" " /89	
...	PLATE,BUTT,ASSEMBLED	*	" 8595		1	" " /G	Also for Rifles Nos.1 and 2
21	PLATE			Br.	1	" " /40A	
22	TRAP	*	" 8636	Br.	1	" " /84	
23	PIN	*	" 8592	St.	1	" " /34	
24	SPRING...	*		St.	1	" " /78	To be demanded under Rifles No.1 (Cat.No. BB 0762)
25	SCREW	*		St.	1	" " /64	To be demanded as Screws, spring, bolt,locking, BB 8614
26	SCREW,plate,butt	*	" 8613	St.	2	" " /61	
27	SCREW,swivel	*	" 8037	St.	3	" " /65	Two only required if bracket, Mk.II and Swivel, sling, Mk.II are used. For Sling, swivel and bands upper, also for Rifles, Nos.1,2 & 3.

Plate J

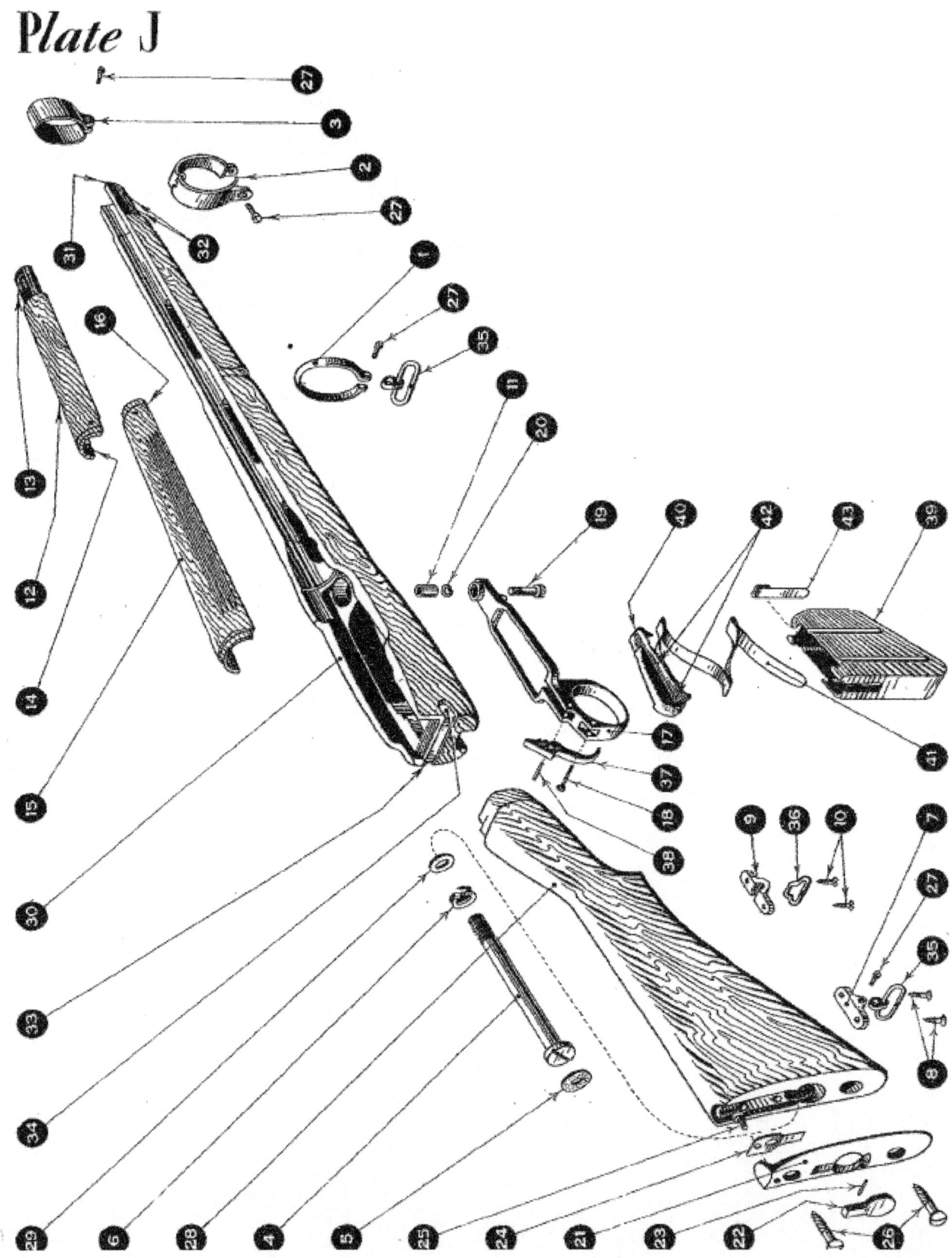
27
3
2
27
31
32
1
27
35
16
11
20
19
40
42
43
39
13
12
14
15
30
33
34
17
41
37
18
38
9
36
10
7
27
35
8
29
6
28
4
5
25
24
21
23
22
26

NO.	DESIGNATION		VOCAB. NO.	MAT.	NO. OFF	DRAWING NO.	
...	RIFLE,NO.4,MK.I & M.I*,.303-in. (con....)						
J28	STOCK,butt						With Stock bolt washer
...	LONG	*	BB 8629		1	DD(E)450/80	
...	NORMAL	*	" 8630		1	" " /80	
...	SHORT	*	" 8631		1	" " /80	
29	WASHER,bolt,stock	*		St.	1	" " /87	To be demanded under Rifles, No.1 (Cat.No.BB 0778
30	STOCK,fore-end,Assd.	*	" 8632		1	" " /H	
31	CAP	*	" 8573	St.	1	" " /13C	
32	PIN	*	" 8594	St.	2	" " /31A	
33	TIE-PLATE			St.	1	" " /42	
34	RIVET...			Br.	1	" " /37A	
35	SWIVEL,sling,Mk.I....	*	" 8043	St.	2	" " /82A	One only required if Swivel,sling,Mk.II is used
36	SWIVEL,sling,Mk.II...	*	" 8671	St.	1	" " /94	Not required if Bracket Mk.I is used
37	TRIGGER	*	" 8638	St.	1	" " /85	
38	PIN	*		St.	1	" " /38	To be demanded as Pins, sear (Cat.No. 8591)
...	RIFLE,NO.4						
...	MAGAZINE,ASSD.	*	" 8029		1	" " /F	
39	CASE	*	" 8572	St.	1	" " /14A	
...	PLATFORM,ASSD.	*	" 8597	St.	1		
40	PLATFORM			St.	1	" " /43	With spring Assd.
41	SPRING			St.	1	" " /75	
42	RIVET			St.	2	" " /46	
43	SPRING,auxiliary...	*	" 8622	S.S.	1	" " /68	

Plate K

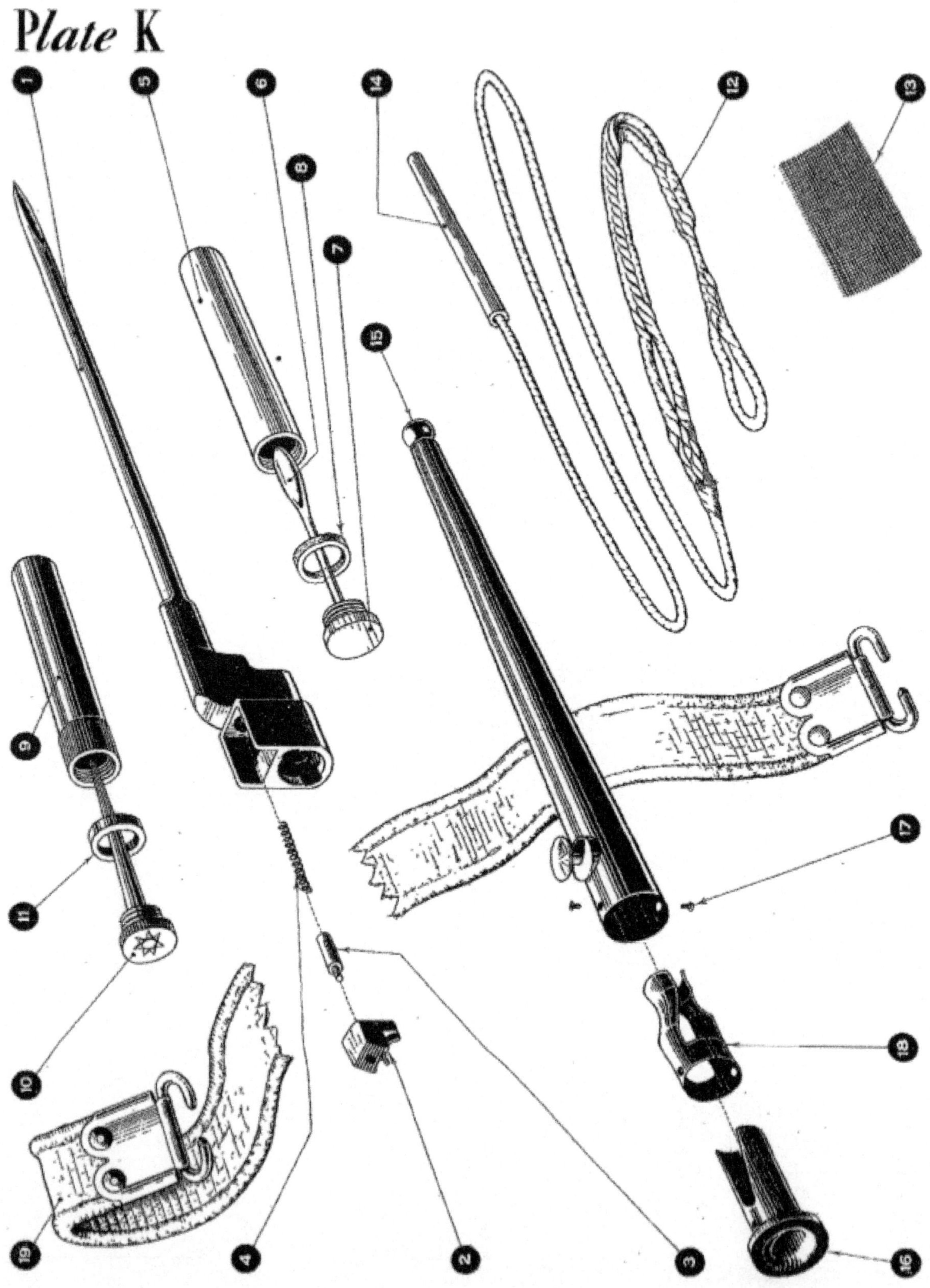

[illegible]	[illegible]		[illegible]	[illegible]	[illegible]	[illegible]	[illegible]
..	BAYONET,NO.4,MKS.II AND II*	*	HA 6260		1	DD(E)2605	Alt. to Mk.II*
		*	HA 6261		1	DD(E)2679	Alt. to Mk.II
1	BLADE		BB 6265	St.	1	" " /1	
2	CATCH	*	" 6252	St.	1	DD(E)340B/2	
3	PLUNGER	*	" 6253	St.	1	" " /3	
4	SPRING	*	" 6254	S.S.	1	" " /4	
..	BOTTLE,OIL,MK.IV	*	BA 0053		1		
5	BODY			Br.	1	ADD(S)360	
6	SPOON	*	BB 0054	St.	1	" 357	
7	STOPPER	*	" 0055	Br.	1	" 358	
8	WASHER	*	" 0056	L.	1	" 359	
..	or BOTTLE,OIL,MK.V		BA 6320			DD(E)2562	
9	BODY			P.M.	1	" " /1	
10	STOPPER,with rod	*	" 6321	P.M.	1	" " /4	
11	WASHER	*	" 6326	L.	1	" " /3	
..	PULL-THROUGH,SINGLE,MK.IV					SAID 2573	
..	"A"		" 0517		1	" "	With wire gauze
..	"B"		" 0518		1	" "	Without wire gauze
12	CORD,single	*	BB 0520	Cord.	1	" "	
13	GAUZE	*	" 0521	St.	1	" "	
14	WEIGHT	*	" 0522	Br.	1	" "	
..	SCABBARD,BAYONET,NO.4	*	BA 8354			DD(E)463B	
15	BODY		BB 8321	St.	1	" " /A	
16	MOUTHPIECE	*	" 8322	St.	1	" " /2	
17	SCREW	*	" 8323	St.	2	" " /3	
18	SPRING	*	" 8324	St.	1	" " /4	
19	SLING,rifle,web		AA 1657	Cws.	1		

Plate L

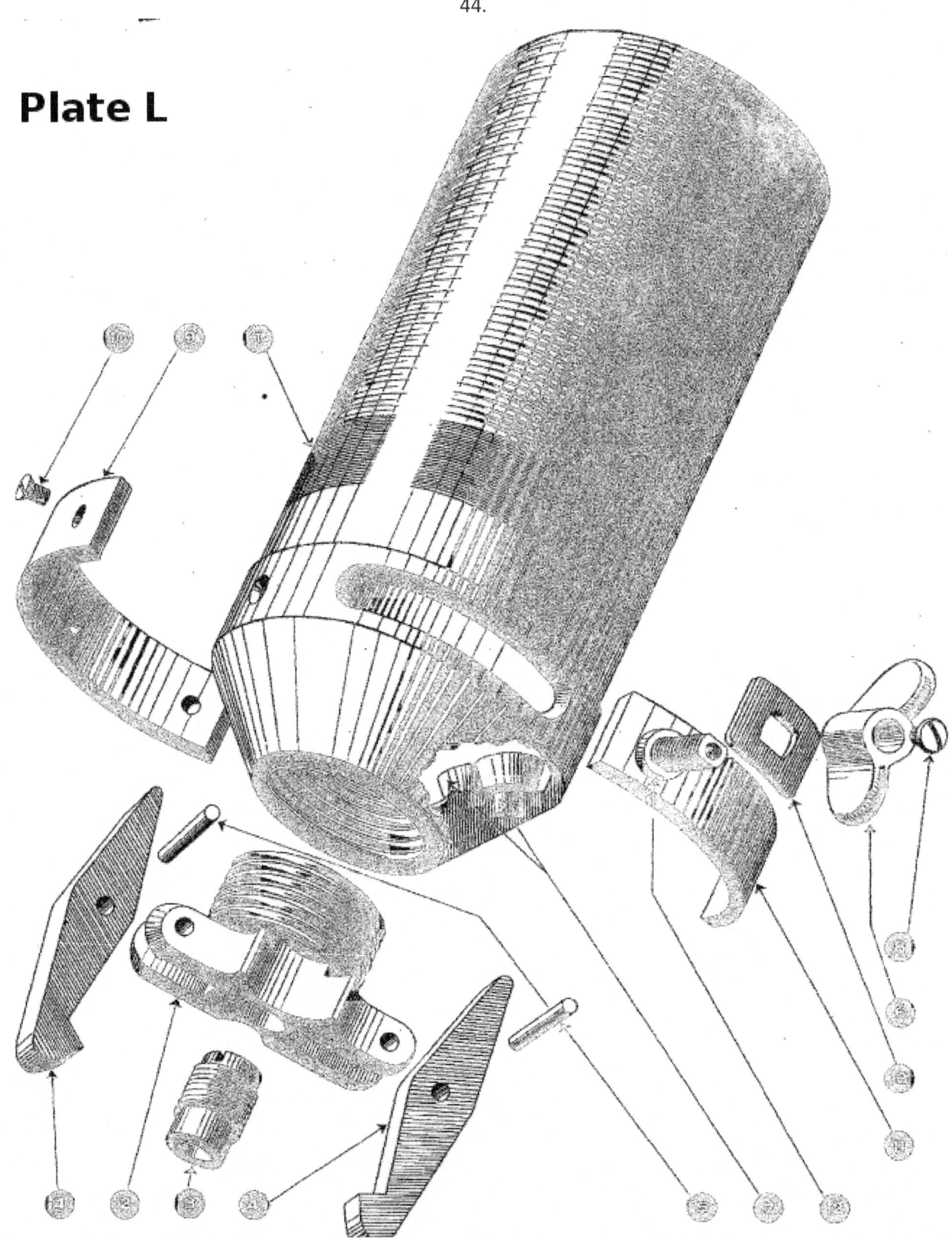

DISCHARGER, GRENADE, RIFLE, No. 1, Mk.I, 2½-in.

REF. NO.	DESIGNATION	VOCAB. NUMBER	MAT.	NO. OFF	DRAWING NUMBER
...	DISCHARGER, GRENADE, RIFLE, NO.1, MK.I, 2-1/2"	BA.0100 GA			A.I.D.1434/C
1	BARREL		M.S.	1	" "
2	BASE		M.S.	1	" "
3	SCREW, adjusting		M.S.	1	" "
4	LEVER		M.S.	2	" "
5	PIN		St.	2	" "
6	NUT, wing, B.S.W., 3/16"	G1/GAA.5852	M.S.	1	" "
7	PEG, steel		M.S.	2	" "
8	SCREW, keep		M.S.	1	" "
9	SEGMENT, fixed		M.S.	1	" "
10	SCREW, fixing (or) Rivet		M.S.	3	" "
11	SEGMENT, moving		M.S.	1	" "
12	STUD, screwed		M.S.	1	" "
13	WASHER		S.S.	1	" "

Numerical Index:

Numerical Index (cont.)

Printed in Great Britain
by Amazon

50874801R00031